WESTERN RESERVE HIGH SCHOOL
LIBRARY

How To Succeed at

SOCCER

How To Succeed At

SOCCER

Gerhard Bauer

PUBLISHING CO., INC. NEW YORK

First published in the United States of America in 1982 by Sterling Publishing Co., Inc., Two Park Avenue, New York, NY 10016

Translated from the German by Beverley Worthington

© BLV Verlagsgesellschaft mbH, Munich 1980

First published in Great Britain by
Orbis Publishing Limited, London 1982

All rights reserved. No part of this publication may be reproduced, stored in a retrieval system, or transmitted, in any form or by any means, electronic, mechanical, photocopying, recording or otherwise, without the prior permission of the publishers. Such permission, if granted, is subject to a fee depending on the nature of the use.

ISBN: 0-8069-4148-0

Printed in Singapore

Contents

The history of soccer 8
Equipment 14
Sporting objectives 16
Technique 17
  Instep kick 20
  Volley kick 24
  Kicking with the inside of the foot 26
  Kicking with the inside instep 30
  Kicking with the outside instep 32
  Heading the ball 34
  Formation exercises 38
  Trapping the ball 40
  Tackling 46
  Feinting and dribbling 52
Fitness and condition 58
  Training methods 62
  Training plans 64
  Training means 66
Tactics 74
  Marking 76
  Systems of play 80
  Team positions 82
  Playing groups 84
  Special situations in the 86
  Tactics on the day 88
Sporting injuries 90
  Methods of treatment 92
Rules of the game 98
The winners 111
Famous names in the game 117
Famous players in the United States 127

Foreword

Soccer, or association football, is one of the world's major leisure-time sports. From youngsters to grandads with hearing aids, teenagers of both sexes, mothers of hopeful young players, grown-ups of all ages and professional groups – all are captivated every weekend by the sport. It is played and enjoyed by millions; and it entices hundreds of thousands of spectators into professional football stadiums, and also attracts all those loyal supporters of amateur teams.

In addition, it is compelling viewing on television, rousing school children, workmates, pubgoers and many others to heated discussions about scored and unscored goals.

Soccer can bring the family together – or divided it, particularly when opinions clash or when a member of the family does not understand anything about the sport or quite simply does not want to know anything

about it. The fascination of the sport can become a hobby of many facets for the whole family, a hobby that can completely fill the free time of its followers.

I have written this book for all those who number soccer – be it as players or spectators – among their hobbies and would like to know more about the sport. A hobby can only be fully enjoyed when you have mastered the theory and practice of it.

The book shows in words and illustrations what a player has to master to be successful and how the technical and tactical elements of the game can be improved by practice and training. For the football lover the book describes how this competitive sport has developed from football-like games of earlier days and how it is played now. It shows that the tactics are not as full of secrets as is often suggested, and explains the rules of the game. One section shows how the whole family can use soccer for keeping fit. Some pages are devoted to the most famous managers and players in the world.

The history of soccer

From early times to the 19th century

The modern game is about 120 years old. However, for several thousand years people have been mastering the art of kicking a ball with their feet. Written evidence of a passion for football has been handed down from a number of races and cultures, to some extent even from pre-Christian times. From old tomb paintings we know that in Egypt about 2000 BC they were kicking a ball about.

The rules of Ts'uh Cow have been handed down intact. We know soccer was played in the 3rd century BC by the Chinese emperor's soldiers. A leather sphere filled with feathers and hair was used as a ball. It had to be kicked into baskets, similar to those in basketball today. In AD 500-600 the game of Kemari was first described in Japan and is still played there on ritual occasions. The ball is revered as a symbol of the sun, and this is reflected in the way in which the game is played. The players stand in a circle and try ingeniously to keep the ball in the air with their feet.

In Ancient Greece and the Roman Empire there were, of course, games similar to soccer. The game of Episkyros has been handed down from the Greeks and from the Romans, the games of Harpastum and Calcio. The Romans certainly brought these games with them to Britain during their campaigns.

In England and Scotland, a tremendous passion for the game grew up between the 8th and 19th centuries. Rough, to some extent undisciplined, games were played between whole villages and small towns, where the ball was thrown about and kicked across streets and town squares. Passion for the game was so great that young people neglected their work and studies. In the 14th and 15th centuries prohibitions against 'useless' football were pronounced by the Lord Mayor of London and by various English and Scottish kings. Nevertheless, as the following chapter shows, the development of the game in England and Scotland could in no way be stopped.

The history of soccer

Development in the 19th century

Whereas the early phases of development of football have largely been handed down piecemeal, the game in modern times has been documented in detail.

The cradle of today's game is in England. A plethora of football-like games were developed in some of the famous English public schools, such as Eton, Harrow and Winchester, and made part of the curriculum. At Rugby, Dr Thomas Arnold first established set rules in 1846. Here the opponent could be tackled in a rough manner and the ball carried by hand. In other schools only stopping the ball by hand was allowed; this was necessary because today's technical skills had not yet been full developed.

After long discussions and heated arguments, 11 London clubs and schools met in the Freemason's Tavern on October 26, 1863 and founded the Football Association, the first soccer association in the world. On December 8 of that year there was a final break with the advocates of rugby, who founded their own association. From this time the game developed in leaps and bounds. By 1871 in England 50 clubs were already contesting a championship trophy.

The history of soccer

In 1872, England and Scotland played the first match between two countries. In 1882 the International Board was founded, which still today – as the highest ruling authority – decides all disputes on questions of rules. As early as 1885, professional soccer was established in England. In 1889, the first non-British associations were founded in Holland and Denmark, following the founding of the Scottish Association in 1873, the Welsh Association in 1875 and the Irish Association in 1880. In 1904, seven countries united to form the 'Fédération Internationale de Football Association' (FIFA) in Paris. In 1930, the first world cup took place in Uruguay.

The development of soccer in Britain

When the four home countries – England, Scotland, Wales and Ireland – formed their own associations, there were no club competitions as such and no professional players. It was very much the age of the amateur and most matches were no more than recreational.

The FA Cup was first played for in 1871-2 and the prestige of the competition grew so quickly that clubs were enticing good players – many of them from Scotland – with cash and work incentives. The FA could not ignore these moves and inevitably had to acknowledge professional status in 1885.

To pay these new professionals, there had to be more football – and, of course, crowds. So the Football League was founded in 1888. The Scots set up their league in 1890; they had already developed a knock-out competition along the same lines as the English. Three years later their association too was forced to accept professionalism.

Politics was the problem that dictated the course of Irish soccer, after an association had been formed in 1880 – and a cup competition the same year. In 1890 the Irish League was set up, but it lasted only 31 years. The

The history of soccer

Argentinian captain Passarella holds the World Cup trophy aloft in 1978.

split, due to political troubles and to World War I, led to the eventual setting up of the FA of Ireland (represented by the Republic of Ireland) and the Irish FA (represented by Northern Ireland).

Wales had different – and, in comparison, minor – problems. For example, it nearly went broke when it started the Welsh Cup in 1877. The league was formed in 1902, but has never been as strong as the other national leagues in Britain. In fact, the top Welsh clubs play in the English League.

Amalgamation of the various football associations to form a single 'Great Britain' side has always been resisted, despite the fact that many of the other British countries' good players spend each season in the English League with English clubs and that there has been mounting criticism in some quarters of the Home International Championships, which are held at the end of a gruelling season every year.

The history of soccer

The development of football in the United States

Surprisingly soccer took a long time to catch on in the United States, despite the fact that a kind of football was being played early in the 19th century. Even in Canada the game had been introduced by Scottish immigrants in about 1880. American Football, which of course is totally distinct from soccer, has for a long time been the dominant game in the United States.

The first national grouping – the American Football Association – was set up in 1884, but was later disbanded. In 1913, it was succeeded by the United States Soccer Football Association. Although professional soccer was then encouraged, it never had the same financial success as its European counterparts and petered out in the Depression.

Immigrants did much to keep it going – and it was a United States team including a number of these that caused one of the great upsets of all time. In 1950 in the World Cup in Brazil they beat England 1-0 at Belo Horizonte.

The resurgence of professional soccer probably coincided with the televising of the 1966 World Cup in England. Within a year two leagues had been formed – the National Professional Soccer League and the North American Soccer League (later the United Soccer Association).

In 1968 these two joined forces to found a 17-strong North American Soccer League. The NASL did not set the soccer scene alight, although the sport was growing in popularity, particularly in schools.

It was not until 1977 that soccer really took off. A staggering 77,000 fans watched the New York Cosmos in one match at the Giants stadium. This new-found popularity was in the main due to the introduction of such foreign stars as Pele, Best and Beckenbauer. The New York Cosmos lured Pele out of retirement in 1975 and two years later Beckenbauer joined him. The pair were not only crowd-pullers; they also helped the Cosmos to the league title.

The game in the United States adopts a different points system from that in Britain. Extra periods are played at the end of a drawn match, followed by a tie-breaker if the scores are still level. This way the draw has been abolished. Other differences include a 35-yard offside line and the use of synthetic turf.

Equipment

If you want to go in for soccer in a competitive way, there is a minimum amount of equipment you should have. Obviously there is a great range with each item, but the figures given here are based on average prices.

You can buy the basic equipment for about £38 (or $80 in the U.S.). For a complete set of equipment with track suit and sports bag you will have to spend nearly twice as much.

Footwear

Boots (shoes in the U.S.) with pile layered soles are all-round footwear to suit any conditions.

In the case of boots designed to take screw-in studs (or cleats), the studs are made of rubber (for hard ground), leather (for snow and ice) or plastic and aluminium (for grass). These can be screwed in according to the weather and ground conditions.

Jersey and shorts

These clothes should allow the player sufficient freedom of movement and be absorbent. In cooler weather cotton jerseys with long sleeves are preferable. The shorts should be cut sufficiently wide. You can now buy them with very practical sewn-in underparts.

Protective devices

Soccer is a hard, competitive sport in which minor injuries can to a great extent be avoided by the wearing of protective clothing. Shin guards, sold in various shapes, are indispensable and plastic models, which are especially light, have proved to be very suitable. Combined shin and

ankle guards are also available.

Players prone to injury should protect their ankle and knee joints with bandages or bandage-type rubber stockings as a precaution. Particularly at the top levels of the game, abdominal protectors should also be worn.

Equipment

Equipment for

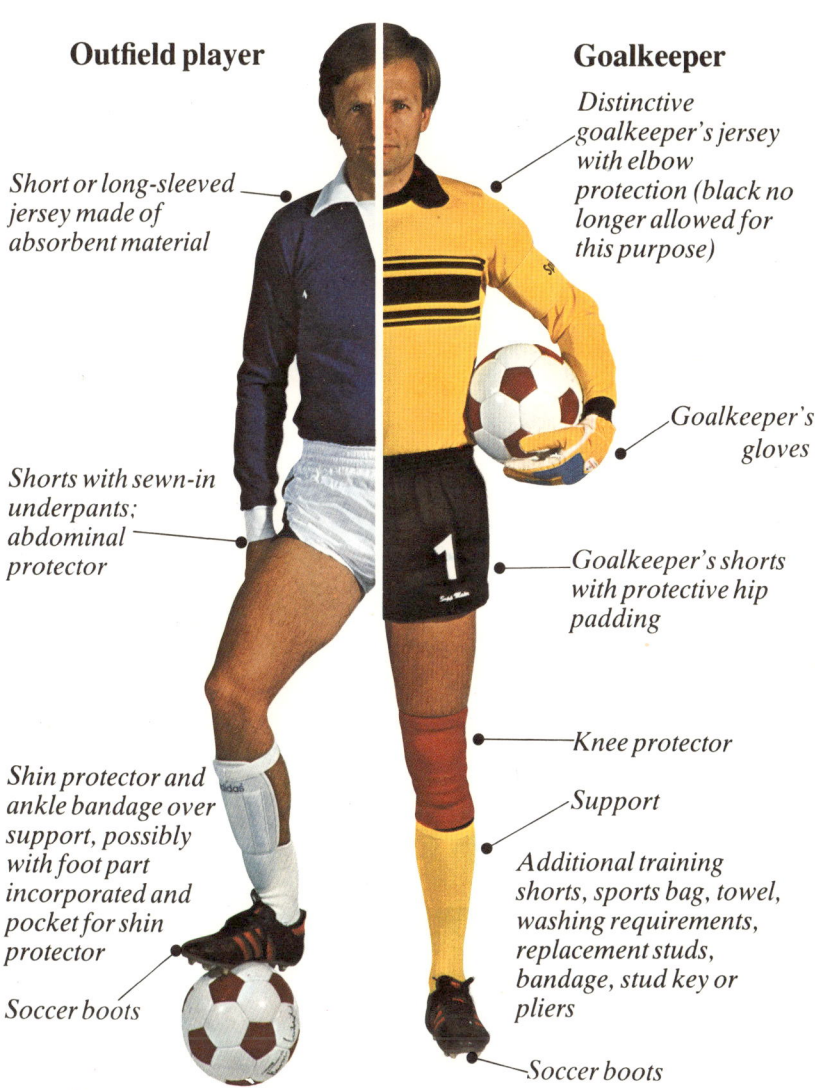

Outfield player

Short or long-sleeved jersey made of absorbent material

Shorts with sewn-in underpants; abdominal protector

Shin protector and ankle bandage over support, possibly with foot part incorporated and pocket for shin protector

Soccer boots

Goalkeeper

Distinctive goalkeeper's jersey with elbow protection (black no longer allowed for this purpose)

Goalkeeper's gloves

Goalkeeper's shorts with protective hip padding

Knee protector

Support

Additional training shorts, sports bag, towel, washing requirements, replacement studs, bandage, stud key or pliers

Soccer boots

Sporting objectives

The game can be played in a free and easy way without any great ambitions or major objectives. But it can also be played by top-class amateurs and professionals with the greatest ambitions. Between these two extremes there are numerous intermediate stages covering a range of objectives.

Total fulfilment in football is always based on three factors:
- technique
- fitness
- tactics

Players who are ambitious must work hard to improve these three aspects of their ability to play the sport. A certain willingness to achieve objectives related to the sport must accompany talent in the conventional sense (that of the technically gifted player). Next to ball sense and a feeling for the game, the following qualities distinguish the successful players of the future from the rest:
- will power
- courage
- tenacity
- stamina
- fighting spirit
- sporting way of life

Only those who have these qualities will be suited to meet the demanding requirements of this ambitious sport. Just how demanding the training requirements for professional players are is indicated in the following table:

Achievements of West German Federal League Players

Running, jumping, starting to run	Defender	Midfield player	Sweeper	Centre forward	Average
Walking	1636 m	2021 m	1689 m	1795 m	1421 m
Trotting	2960 m	3010 m	2801 m	3054 m	2521 m
Run/medium	843 m	512 m	639 m	452 m	568 m
Run/fast	317 m	418 m	175 m	208 m	219 m
Run/maximum	100 m	166 m	163 m	177 m	143 m
Run total/m	5856 m	6127 m	3778 m	5742 m	4466 m
Jumping	8 times	3 times	4 times	6 times	5 times
Starting to run	27 times	28 times	14 times	77 times	36 times
Stopping from max. run	16	not recorded	6	15	12

Technique

Technique as the first and most important factor in competitive achievement is far more than just acrobatic self-expression.

Technique is all-important in competitive football. It allows the demands of competition to be met by means of single-minded, economical skills. At this level of the game players have very complex, technical demands made on them. Unlike a juggler who can concentrate fully on the ball, applying technique and skill, the footballer must be able to fend off the challenge of an opponent and simultaneously keep a look-out for the best possible passes as he receives the ball or is about to pass it. Therefore in the modern game technical skills must be mastered at high and maximum speeds.

The adjoining table is the result of some research done by students at the Munich Technical University on a selection of league matches in Germany, showing how frequently individual techniques are used by midfield players at this level of the game. The comparisons are of interest wherever the game is played.

Naturally you should not over-react to them or overestimate the importance of those techniques that show up much more than others – in their own way all are important. Technique should not become an end in itself but should be, like condition and tactics, a method used by players according to different situations of play.

It is amazing that even strikers are not usually in possession of the ball for more than 3 minutes in a game. However they are on the move for 87 minutes, passing to their team-mates or chasing after the ball – or an opponent with it.

Frequency of use of different techniques

Technique	Frequency
Receiving short pass	38
Receiving long pass	9
One-two	10
1-15m pass	38
15-30m pass	15
Pass over 30m	2
Dribbling (with opponent)	9
Shot at goal from 16-yard line	2
Shot at goal from second line of attack	2
Centering from right/left	4
Header	1
Corner kick	
Front block tackle	7
Accelerating tackle	1
Charging tackle	1
Side block tackle	6
Straddle-legged tackle	3
Sliding tackle	1
Close passing	14
Diagonal passing	40
Narrow-angled passing	13
Kicking the ball	211
Chasing an opponent	275

These averages for midfield players were taken from four league matches in West Germany

Technique

Body technique

Body technique is the mastery of body movements in all conceivable situations as a foundation for controlling the ball.

A player must be able to run forwards, backwards and sideways, start off and sprint. He must be able to jump for the ball and use his whole body effectively for power headers. In dribbling and tackling he ought to be able to twist as fast as lightning and turn, and he must be able to stop and start constantly. Finally, by perfecting a fall technique, he will avoid many of the injuries that occur from challenges with other players.

Ball technique

Only players who control their bodies in the above-described manner can express their feeling for the ball effectively using good ball technique.

The elements of ball technique can be broken down as follows:
- stopping the ball, today thought of as more important than taking possession of the ball and running with it
- aiming and hitting the ball
- dribbling the ball
- taking the ball off an opponent – tackling

Aiming and hitting
With the inside of the foot – outside of the foot – instep – sole

Dribbling/feinting
Feinting with the ball
Feinting with the eyes
Body feinting

Starting to run – running – sprinting
Forwards – backwards – sideways

Stopping and running off with the ball using head – chest – thigh – stomach – inner/outer side of foot – instep – sole

Playing the ball using head – instep – inside of instep – inside of foot – knee

Ball technique

Football techniques

Body technique

Getting possession

Jumping – hopping – twisting – stopping – turning

Sliding tackles

Instep kick

Technique: the foot, hip and knee joints of the supporting leg should be flexible. The kicking leg swings through, whipping forwards with the hip and knee joints in a straight line. At the moment of contact with the ball, there should be a foot's distance between the supporting leg and the ball. The ankle of the kicking foot should be stretched out and rigid. The point of contact should be the instep of the laces and the upper part of the body should at that stage be bent over the ball.

Suitable for: short pass ✓
long pass ✓
low pass ✓
high ball ✓
hard shot at goal ✓
placed shot at goal ✓
bending the ball

Individual training
1 Hold out the ball and kick it high in the air, with foot outstretched and knee bent, and catch it again; also do this over a rope or rod.
2 Kick the ball against a wall from distances of from 3 to 4 metres, and later on from 6 to 8 metres. Kick without stopping the ball.

Training with a partner
1 Try to shoot at goal from 8 to 10 metres, with the other player defending the goal. Try holding the ball at hip height and kicking it using the full instep.
2 Soccer tennis. Pass the ball to your partner at waist height; also do this over a rope, bush or something similar. Alter the distance between players.

Training in a group
1 Punch the ball as high and far as possible in the air to your opponent (later on directly to him) down a long, narrow pitch (approximately 40 x 100 metres). Your opponent should kick it back from where he caught it.
2 Play handball soccer with two teams into two goals (see page 79).

Typical mistakes: direction of the run-up, direction of the kicking movement or supporting leg not pointing at the target
• ankle joint not rigid • supporting leg too far from the ball
• kicking leg not bent enough at the knee • upper part of the body not over the ball.

Instep kick

The full instep kick can be used in many ways in a game; short and long, flat and high, gentle and hard passes can all be played using it. This type of kick is especially suitable for shooting at goal because of the maximum contact on the ball achieved by using the full instep.

Although the sequence of movements after the instep kick is not complicated, you must repeat the kick frequently in training, partly because of the relatively small area of contact on the foot. You must kick very accurately with the instep if the ball is to reach its target. This is only possible with constant practice in varied situations close to those of actual play. The pass and the resulting situation before the shot at goal should be varied as follows:
- forward ground pass
- high forward pass
- alternate ground and high passes from the left and right
- pass from behind
- instep kick after aiming and kicking the ball ahead
- instep kick after dribbling from a turn

Shooting at goal using the instep kick should be done early, even when under pressure from an opponent. In this way the opponent can firstly make a dummy challenge and then challenge for real later on.

Volley kick

Technique: Swing the kicking leg out horizontally from the hip joint in a semi-circular movement towards the ball. The supporting leg is twisted in the direction of the kick by the swinging movement of the kicking leg. The kicking foot and the point of contact are as for the full instep kick. Tip the upper part of the body sideways, so it is almost horizontal, to balance yourself.

Suitable for:
- short pass
- long pass ✓
- low pass
- high pass ✓
- hard shot at goal ✓
- placed shot at goal
- bending the ball

Individual training
1. Stretching and strengthening the trunk muscles by swinging your leg over a chair.
2. Using your right and left leg alternately, kick the ball 2 to 3 metres to the right and then to the left in front of you.

Training with a partner
1. Volley the ball to and fro to your partner over 30 to 40 metres, firstly throwing the ball high up with your hand and then kicking it, and later without catching it.
2. Player A in goal throws the ball high to player B, who is about 11 metres away. B volleys at goal. Change round after five goes.

Training in a group
1. Four players – one ball: A throws or centres from 10-30 metres on one side. B volleys. C is the goalkeeper and D fetches the ball. After each shot, change round positions.
2. Five men – one ball: the arrangement is as above (1), but the extra player is on the opposite side to cross the ball from the other direction. Cross from right and left alternately.

Typical mistakes: upper part of the body does not lean far enough to the side • the hip-swinging movement comes too late and is not high enough • ankle joint bent • ankle joint not rigid • not enough mobility in the hip joint.

Kicking with the inside of the foot

Technique: Turn the kicking leg outwards from the hip joint, with the knee and foot bent. Make sure the inside of the kicking foot faces towards the direction of play, draw the toes upwards and keep the foot rigid at the ankle joint. The point of contact is the inside of the foot from the beginning of the toes to the ankle.

Suitable for:
- short pass ✓
- long pass
- low pass ✓
- high pass ✓
- hard shot at goal
- placed shot at goal ✓
- bending the ball ✓

Individual training
1. Work out with both feet using a soccer trainer (if you have one) or against a wall.
2. Taking penalty kicks accurately: aim to place the ball about 25cm inside the post.

Training with a partner
1. Soccer tennis over a rope, fence or hedge, for example.
2. Combination exercises (see page 38) to increase distances and running speed, at first just receiving the ball and later on passing it.

Training in a group
1. Three to six players – several balls: the players run in a circle around the goal at a distance of 10 metres, passing the balls to one another using the inside of the foot; the player in the most advantageous position shoots at goal, when passed to, using the inside of the foot.
2. Three against one, four against two, five against three, etc: the players with the balls stand in a triangle, square or circle and pass to one another using the inside of the foot. The players in the middle try to intercept the balls.

Typical mistakes: kicking leg not turned out enough • toes not drawn up enough • loose ankle joint • knee and ankle joint not rigid at the time of the kick • the toes of the supporting leg not pointing in the direction of play.

Kicking with the inside of the foot

Kicking with the inside of the foot is the safest and most accurate way of kicking the ball. It is therefore especially good for knocking on balls, for accurate passes and for placing shots at goal from a distance. Balls falling from a height can either be played along the ground or in the air. In the latter case, the ball is played as a half-volley, ie it is kicked at the exact moment it bounces up off the ground.

If you do not kick the ball with the inside of the foot exactly in the middle but to one side, you may give the ball spin. Then its flight path is no longer straight, but more or less arched. By hitting to one side of the ball, you can to an extent pass round an opponent and prevent him reaching the ball. Using this technique, the ball can also be hit with the inside or outside of the instep. These are the master skills

Technique

of passing.

You can also vary the height of the flight path of the ball to suit different situations of play. With ground play, keep your supporting leg next to the ball and the upper part of the body over the ball. Playing a high ball, your supporting leg should be behind the ball and the upper part of the body should be leaning backwards.

In the above sequence of pictures the player is taking care to play the ball as low as possible.

Points to note:
- *have your supporting leg next to the ball*
- *have the upper part of your body over the ball*
- *hit the ball at or about the middle*

Run after the ball when you have kicked it. If any one of these points has not been observed, you will kick the ball higher than intended.

Kicking with the inside instep

Technique: The run-up to the ball should be at an angle of approximately 45°. The supporting leg should be three foot-widths away from the ball and bent sharply. The kicking leg should be turned slightly outwards at the hip joint and knee. The toes of the kicking foot should be somewhat raised (roughly between the position for the instep kick and the inside of the foot kick). The point of contact should be the inner edge of the instep. The upper part of the body should be leaning sideways over the pivoting leg.

Suitable for: short pass
long pass ✓
low pass
high pass ✓
hard shot at goal ✓
placed shot at goal ✓
bending the ball ✓

Individual training
1 Shot at goal bending the ball around a small flag.
2 Try to bend the ball when taking corners to score direct.

Training with a partner
1 A is on the wing, B is centre forward; B plays from the halfway line to A, who hits the ball along the touchline and centres from the dead-ball line to B, who has been running parallel to A. B shoots at goal.
2 A and B bend the ball over approximately 30 metres to one another around a small flag; alternate between ground and high passes.

Training in a group
1 Three players – one ball: the players run round an imaginary circle of approximately 30 metres in diameter and centre the ball, on the run, to the man in front or the one behind.
2 Four players – one ball: arrangement in a rectangle with sides of 5 and 26 metres. A makes a short ground pass to B, who is 5 metres away; B centres to C, who kicks a short pass directly to D; he centres back to A, and so on.

Typical mistakes: run-up too straight so that the ball is struck off-centre • pivoting leg too near the ball, bending it as above • pivoting leg too far from the ball • upper part of the body leans too far backwards, therefore resulting in too weak a shot • kicking leg not turned out enough.

Kicking with the outside instep

Technique: The run-up should be slightly curved (with a kick using the right leg from the right). The supporting leg should be bent and two foot-widths away from the ball. The kicking leg should be turned slightly inwards at the hip joint and knee. The point of contact is the outer edge of the instep from the joints to the ankle. The upper part of the body should lean slightly forwards towards the side of the supporting leg.

Suitable for: short pass ✓
long pass ✓
low pass ✓
high pass ✓
hard shot at goal ✓
placed shot at goal ✓
bending the ball ✓

Individual training
1 At about 30 metres from goal, take the ball towards goal; at about 20 metres shoot at goal using the outer instep.
2 Work out by kicking against a wall, using the outer instep of the right and left leg alternately.

Training with a partner
1 Zig-zag combinations with and without changing places (see page 38) over short and long distances.
2 Both players positioned next to one another on the halfway line; one kicks the ball in the direction of goal. Both start towards the ball and the quicker one becomes the striker, the other a defender. The striker shields the ball with his body and shoots at goal using the outer instep.

Training in a group
As with the inside of the instep kicks (see page 30).

Typical mistakes: kicking foot not turned far enough inwards, giving too small an area of contact and also a tendency to slice the ball ● run-up too straight ● upper part of body leaning back away from the ball, reducing the power of the shot.

Technique

Remark: The outer instep kick is the most useful of all the types of kick. A high degree of accuracy can be achieved with plenty of power because of the relatively large area of contact. Therefore spend a lot of time perfecting this technique.

In the sequence of photographs you can clearly see how the kicking foot is turned inwards with the outer instep kick. The deeper the curve of the run-up, the more you will bend the ball.

Heading the ball

Technique: The legs should be apart or one in front of the other. The upper of the body is bent backwards and then launched towards the ball. The throat and neck muscles should be tensed. The chin should be lowered down on to the chest. The point of contact is the whole of the forehead or the side of the forehead. (Because of the danger of injury connected with this technique, never in any circumstances use the temples.)

Suitable for: short pass ✓
long pass
low pass ✓
high pass ✓
hard shot at goal
placed shot at goal ✓
bending the ball

Individual training
Keep the ball in the air with your head, first of all standing still and then moving forwards.

Training with a partner
1. The two players stand in mini-goals (made of poles) at about 5 to 10 metres from each other ready for a goal-shooting competition. Each in turn throws the ball in the air and heads it at goal.
2. Player A holds the ball high above his head; B stands underneath the ball, then jumps up, at the same time bending back, and heads towards the held ball.

Training in a group
1. Training for heading at goal (see page 25 for set-up).
2. Alternate play with the ball using head and hands (for example, with six against six in an area that has been marked out with two mini-goal areas). The ball is passed, caught, thrown high in the air and headed on to the next player, who in turn catches it, throws it up, heads it, and so on. Opponents are only allowed to defend with their heads if the ball is at or above chest height.

Typical mistakes: no spring forward after bending back ● heading from a jump with run-up – jumping off from both feet instead of just one ● when jumping off, the jumping leg is not pushed backwards ● neck and throat muscles not tensed during header.

A good heading technique is especially important in today's game. A strong, attacking player who also marks closely will rarely allow his opponent to collect a high ball. The old rule 'never let the ball bounce' was not made for nothing. This works equally well for attackers and defenders. So the ball should be headed on as early as possible. Whoever jumps up first and highest has the best chance of success.

Apart from the straight header from a standing, running or jumping position (see

accompanying sequence of photographs), the variations include glancing headers and flying headers. With the latter, the player dives forwards in an often spectacular manner towards a lowish ball coming towards him. Players have often surprised their opponents with this technique and have scored some great goals with it too.

You ought to begin training for heading early on as well. To prevent injury to the head, children are advised to use a lighter ball.

Formation exercises

The types of kick shown on pages 20-37 can be executed and improved not only by following the specific training methods mentioned, but also through general practice and combination exercises.

The basic tactical skills involved in running off the ball and position changing can be developed at the same time as the technique. After passing, attention should always be paid to accelerating quickly into a run.

Changing position while zig-zagging.

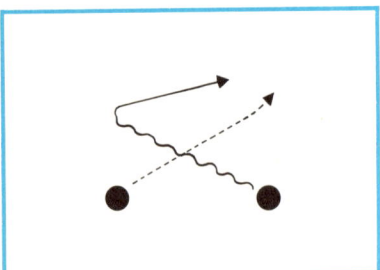

Player A plays the ball diagonally across the pitch; player B switches behind him to the other side. While turning round using the above-mentioned technique, A passes the ball to B who takes the ball while running diagonally (across the pitch) and so on. First of all move at a slow speed, taking the ball with you. Then later increase the speed and pass the ball.

Changing position while attacking – at right angles

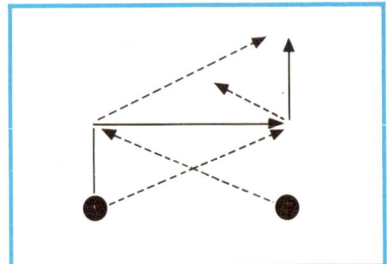

A hits the ball upfield, while B – 10 metres away from him – runs for it at an angle in front of A. A runs behind B's back at an angle to the other side. B passes the ball square to A, then runs diagonally across to the other side, and so on.

Attack – attack

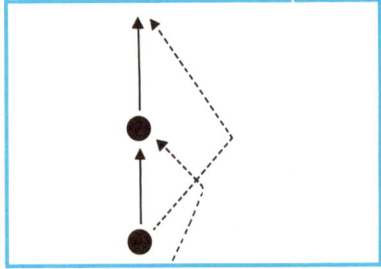

A is positioned behind B on the pitch. A hits a through ball to B; he takes it and waits until A has run past him in an arc before passing it forward. A is now the front player and receives the ball, while B runs past him in an arc and takes the next pass.

Technique

Triangular game without changing position

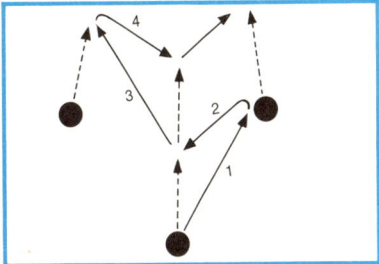

Three players run in a triangular formation. The back player A passes to B on the right and runs upfield. B receives the ball, passes back to A and runs upfield. A takes the ball again and passes it out to C on the left. C, running forward, takes the ball and passes back to A, running through, and so on. The players can change positions after each pass.

Triangular game with position changing

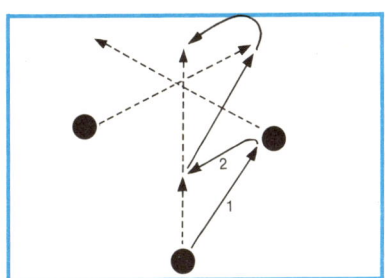

The basic formation is as above. After making a long diagonal pass to B on the right, A moves forward and receives a pass back from B. He then plays the ball out to the right and C runs diagonally to the right to collect it. A continues to run forward to receive a pass back from C, while B crosses over to take up the left-hand position.

Three-man interchange – attack – diagonal

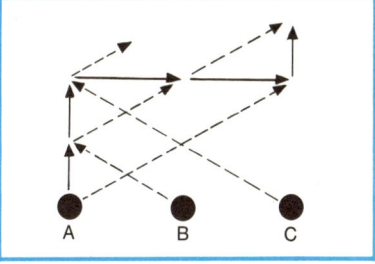

The three players line up in a row. A kicks the ball upfield. B runs diagonally to the left after it and plays it upfield again for C, who has already run diagonally to the left, to collect. He passes it square to the right for B to collect; he in turn passes it square for A to pick up. After contact with the ball, each man changes over position by running at an angle to the right.

Trapping the ball

The trapping technique used in the past in matches and in training has little significance today. Until well into the Sixties, the rule of 'trap, look and pass' was effective enough. On the whole, players brought the ball, which was passed to them, to a complete stop before passing it to a team-mate.

Modern-day players acting as spearheads are mostly outnumbered by the opposing defenders. The space in front of goal is now very cramped due to the number of defenders and each player is usually closely marked by an opponent. If today a player was to trap the ball according to the old rule, he would almost certainly be caught with the ball by an opponent. The player using the new technique feints and takes the ball with him as soon as he receives it.

It is therefore more accurate to talk of 'receiving the ball and taking it with you' than of 'trapping' it. With the principal exception of the hands and forearm, you can take the ball on practically any part of the body. The parts of the body you can use are as follows:
- head
- chest
- stomach
- upper and lower leg
- instep
- outside of the foot
- inside of the foot

Technique

The technique of receiving and taking the ball is basically always the same. The part of the body receiving the ball should be pointing towards the ball. At the moment of contact it draws back and pushes forward in the desired direction. This technique is more effective if the muscles are, as far as possible, relaxed when contact is made with the ball. Therefore always try to take the ball in a relaxed manner.

The sequence of movements is basically the opposite to the corresponding type of kick. There are two different ways of controlling the ball as it hits your chest.
- If you bend the upper part of your body backwards at the moment of contact with the ball, the ball will remain close to your body.
- If you take the ball while you are running forwards, lean the upper part of your body forwards over the ball at the moment of contact and the ball will drop down in front of your legs – and can be played from there.

Technique

Training exercises

Individual training
1 Either punch or kick the ball at least 3 metres up in the air and then run forwards on to it. Use all the techniques in rotation for this and try early on taking the ball while feinting in the opposite direction.
2 Kick the ball very hard against a wall from about 5 to 10 metres and, after the rebound, take it with you to the right, left, forwards and backwards.
3 Run through a zig-zag slalom of poles, about 10 metres apart, throwing the ball towards the one in front of you. Start after it and, the moment it touches the ground, take it round that pole in the direction of the next pole. After running on with it for a short time, throw it to the next pole, and so on.

Training with a partner
1 Use all the combination exercises on page 38; receive and play the ball on before you pass it again.
2 Player A runs backwards, while player B runs forwards in the same direction at a distance of roughly 10 metres. A throws the ball alternately to the right and left of B, who takes it on the run and passes it forward to A. A throws back to B, using the throw-in technique to achieve the kind of pass that would be made in actual play.
3 Player A is roughly at the level of the 6-yard box in front of goal, while player B is positioned about 25 metres from the goal. A passes a hard, low or high ball to B and immediately challenges. B takes over the ball and tries to get round the challenging A by dribbling and finish with a shot at goal.

Training in a group
Up to 10 players stand in a row facing another player, who is about 20 to 40 metres away; the lone player passes high balls to the first player in the row, who starts running towards him. When the latter receives the ball, he passes it back to the lone player and runs into position about 30 metres on the other side of him. Meanwhile the lone player passes the ball to the next player in the row and the latter repeats the movements. And so on.

Trapping the ball

Taking the ball on the inside of the foot

Low and high balls are controlled and played using the inside of the foot. The ball can be controlled running forwards or darting sideways to the right or left. Forwards very frequently bring the ball down while turning up to 180°.

When an opponent challenges the player on the end of a pass, the control and playing-on of the ball are always preceded by a body feint. The double-step combination required for this wastes both time and space.

Taking the ball on the outside of the foot

Low and high balls can be controlled and played using the outside of the foot. This technique is especially suitable when an opponent is making a strong challenge, since the whole body can be put between the ball and the opponent. When using this technique, you should also try to shake off your opponent with a feint prior to controlling the ball. Controlling the ball with the outside of the foot is also important for forwards because they can get a shot in at goal after the first stride forward with the ball.

Technique

Trapping the ball

Taking the ball on the chest

A broad, flexible chest is needed for receiving and controlling high balls successfully. There are two basic techniques for this:
- Lean the upper part of the body backwards at the moment of contact so the ball comes on to the chest and remains close to the body.
- Lean the upper part of the body forwards over the ball so that it drops down to the ground in front of you; you can immediately run forward with the ball at your feet.

Taking the ball on the thigh

If you have enough time and space, you can also take the ball on the thigh. The relatively large surface of the thigh, which is soft and well-muscled, is very suitable for taking the ball – even for the less expert players. It is important that you point the thigh towards the ball early enough, since only then can you successfully reduce the momentum of the ball. This is done by bringing back the thigh.

Technique

Tackling

Since forwards have learnt the art of dribbling to help run through defences, defenders must perfect reliable ways of winning the ball. In the 1954 World Cup, which Germany won, their defenders demonstrated the art of the sliding tackle for the first time. At the time this technique was somewhat derisively called 'the scythe'. Since then the technique has become part of the standard repertoire of every good defender.

The six methods of tackling are as follows:
- front block tackle
- charging tackle
- accelerating tackle
- side block tackle
- straddle-legged tackle
- sliding tackle

The individual methods of tackling are differentiated by the relative positions in which the forward and defender find themselves. With the straddle-legged and sliding tackles, the defender risks losing the ball completely because after the challenge he will be lying on the ground. If the tackle is not effective, he will not be able to chase after the forward to have a second attempt at recovering the ball. Therefore these methods of tackling should be used as a last resort.

Technique

Training exercises

Individual training

Inevitably tackling practice can only be carried out with someone else playing the ball. When training alone, you can only stretch and strengthen the thigh muscles – and those of the inside of the thigh in particular – with gymnastic exercises.
Straddle-legged exercises of a splits-like nature with and without the ball are particularly suitable. With the sliding tackle you make straddling movements as you move round in front of your opponent. As with all other technical skills, you should try tackling with both legs.

Training with a partner

1 A one against one situation into a mini-goal area: the person with the ball becomes the forward, while the other is the defender.
2 Four men – one ball: two players stand with legs well apart at a distance of 10 metres, while the two others play one against one into these mini-goals.
3 Player A plays the ball along the touchline; player B chases him. A tries to centre on the run in the direction of goal and B tries to stop him with a side block tackle.
4 One against one game: one player kicks a through ball from the centre circle; this is covered by a defender. According to the situation, the defender has to decide whether he should try to get to the ball using a front block tackle or whether he should check the run at the moment the forward receives the ball by using a charging tackle. If he arrives too late to use either of these two tackling methods, he must try to separate the striker, who is now coming head-on towards him, from the goal with a straddle-legged tackle.

Training in a group

1 All small games of one against one to six against six are very suitable for tackling practice. In every case it is important that every player is assigned a direct defender. The player who wants to win back the ball must use every opportunity to show aggression when tackling.
2 An 'attack against defence' game into one goal: a defender, who must tackle at the earliest possible opportunity, is assigned to each attacker.

Remark: To avoid most injuries, you should always wear shin guards during tackling training.

Tackling

Front block tackle

The defender places his whole body in the path of the striker. He blocks the ball with the inside of his kicking leg. The ball bounces back from this leg, which should be rigid with all muscles tensed.

1

2

5

4

3

Technique

3

4

5

2

1

Accelerating tackle

In the accelerating tackle the defender is positioned behind the opposing striker – in relation to the ball. From this position the defender can accelerate quickly past the striker and intercept the ball; at the same time he 'shoulder-charges' the opponent.

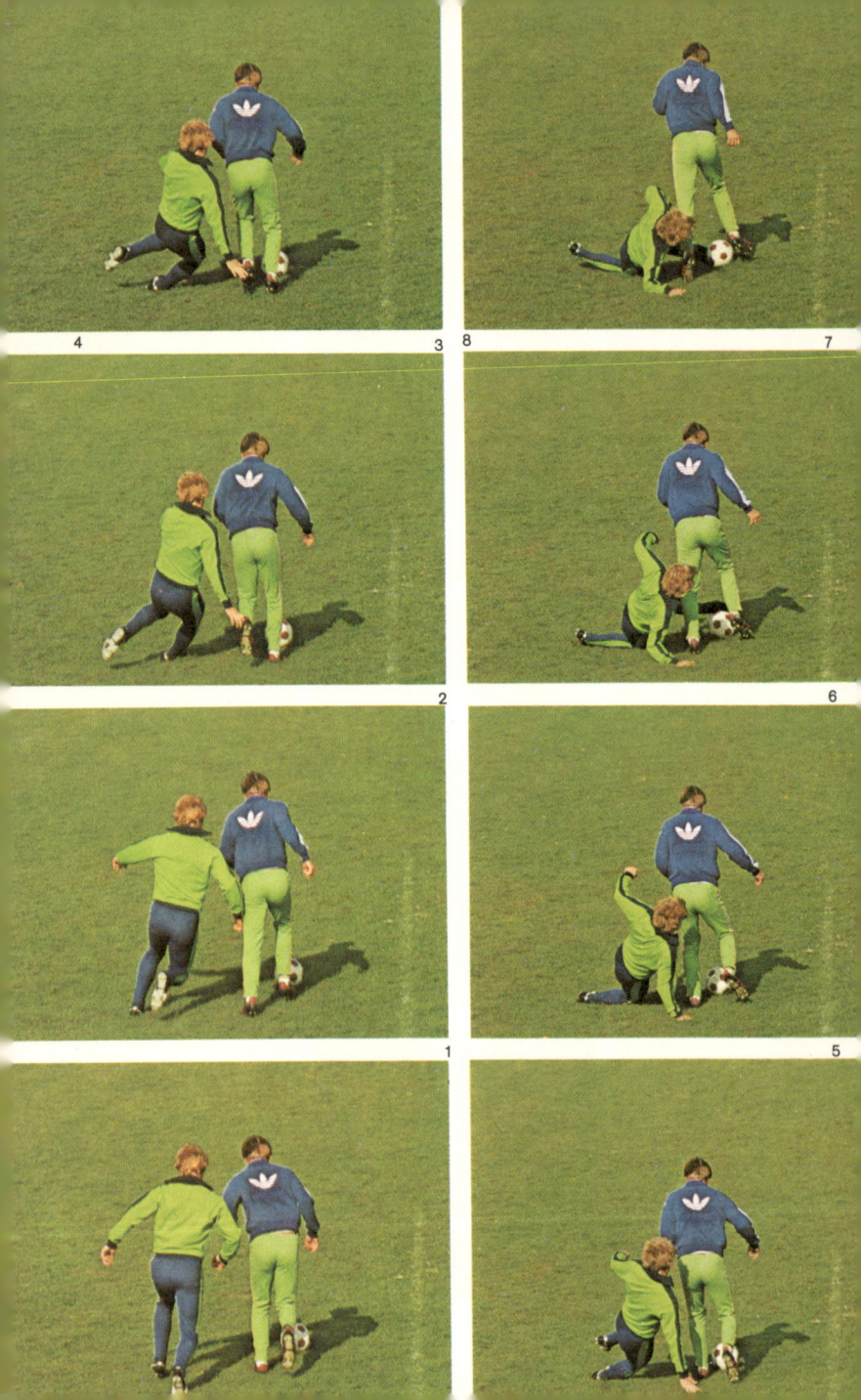

11 12

10

9

Technique

Sliding tackle

The sliding tackle is technically the most difficult and tactically the riskiest method of intercepting the ball. It should, therefore, only be used in emergencies, ie if an opponent has passed the defender and is ready to shoot at goal. In all other cases, you should chase your opponent and, when you have caught up, carry on the struggle for the ball with a shoulder charge.

The following points should be borne in mind for the sliding tackle only:

- the pivoting leg should be well bent at the final step to lower the centre of gravity.
- the kicking leg should always be your outside one, that is the one turned away from the ball. At an angle from behind, slide the foot up to the ball and kick the ball out of the striker's path.
- lean the upper part of your body sideways and balance with your arm.

To avoid cuts and bruises when using the sliding tackle, you should control your momentum by rolling your body lengthways. You will be able to get to your feet more quickly from a rolling movement and therefore get back into action faster.

Feinting and dribbling

In the modern game strikers are usually outnumbered by defenders. This stranglehold can only be broken by the unexpected switch of teamwork with surprise dribbling. Therefore in today's game the good player must also be a good dribbler. What has already been said generally about technique is particularly applicable to dribbling. It should never be an end in itself, but always be used for tactical reasons.

The following basic tactical rules should be followed for dribbling:

- Any pass is better than dribbling the ball, however quick. Therefore only dribble when there is no free player in a good position to pass to. Another suitable situation is where you can gain the best position for shooting at goal through dribbling.
- Dribbling is also used when you want to retain possession of the ball. It is then very difficult for a defender to get to the ball because the player with the ball is not bent on looking for a direct way to goal, but can retreat towards his own goal.
- Apparently aimless playing and dribbling of the ball can temporarily slow down the game and lull your opponents off guard. At a propitious moment you can carry the game forward unexpectedly into the opponents' half using quick passes. This change in tempo is an important tactical element in modern football.
- Finally the man with the ball will have to dribble when a fellow player has run into an offside position; otherwise a pass to him will result in a free kick to the opposition.

Whether dribbling is successful or not depends in the end on the player's speed and any feinting used. There are three types of feint that can be used – body, ball and eye.

Body feint

A feint is made in one direction by a shift in body weight, a suggested shooting movement of the leg or by other more or less obvious movements, the ball then being hit in another direction.

Technique

Ball feint

This is frequently connected with a body feint. To confuse the opponent even more, a feint is made with the ball first played to one side. The opponent is committed to challenging in this direction and then is caught on the wrong foot in the opposite direction to the way the ball is finally kicked.

Eye feint

Cunning strikers, particularly when dealing with experienced defenders who no longer fall for the usual feints, signal a certain action by a glance. If the opponent reacts in the desired manner, the ball can be played in the opposite direction. Eye feints are 'conspicuously inconspicuous'.

Feinting and dribbling

Body feint

Left: while running, step to the right over the ball with your right foot, and then kick the ball away to the left with your left foot.

Right: feint a kick to the left, but kick it to the right with the outside of the instep of the right foot.

Technique

Ball feint

Left: while running forwards, pull back the ball with the side of your foot and, after twisting your body round, kick away to the right or the left with the inside or outside of your foot.

Right: while running, aim the ball to the left with the inside of your foot and then kick it immediately to the right with the outside of your foot.

Feinting and dribbling

Training

The complicated, technical dribbling run should always be learnt as a whole and worked on as such, since there are no suitable preliminary exercises for individual feints. Training details are set out as follows:

- recognising the pre-feinting run-up: the trick should be demonstrated by a professional player, fellow player or trainer. It is ideal if the feint is shown several times in succession.
- try out the trick for yourself: try out the feint without an opponent until the basic run-up movements have been mastered. Complicated feints must be practised many times on different days to this end.
- to make the trick automatic: use a training partner to play against you. He must not make a full challenge, but just a feint challenge. Do the same trick again and again – up to 50 times each training day.
- vary the trick: in small games of one against one to six against six, use the trick you have learnt when an opponent has to be passed or shaken off.

Training exercises

Individual training
1. Try to do as many body and ball feints as possible without an opponent over the course of several weeks and months.
2. Run through a slalom made of small flags on poles, one behind the other, or a forest of small flags on poles positioned at random. Use the different feints alternately, before running round a pole.

Training with a partner
1. Player A tries to keep the ball as long as possible using feints, while player B challenges from all sides. Basic rule for A: keep your body between the man and the ball.
2. One against one game into one goal: player A is the striker, while player B bars the way to goal, initially without challenging strongly. Use all of the feints learned.

Training in a group
1. One against one game into one goal: the forward should cut out the defender using, alternately, a one-two with another player or by dribbling past him.
2. All small-game formations (see page 70): here the man with the ball should first dribble round his opponent before he passes.

Fitness and condition

What condition is in the narrow sense of sporting terminology for the competitive sportsman (ie the basis for ultimate achievement) is fitness for the less serious sportsman. Being fit means being in good shape physically for everyday work-outs, healthy and adaptable. Being in good condition or fit means that you are physically fit and healthy enough to be capable of extra achievement both in sport and in everyday life.

There is little basic difference between fitness and condition. In the case of condition, it is rather a question of being in the right state of mind to compete, in which general fitness is further developed by specific training to suit the type of sport.

The part-time sportsman who would like to improve his fitness, as well as the competitive sportsman who is bothered about his condition, build up their capabilities on the basis set out in the diagram.

Fitness + condition = capability

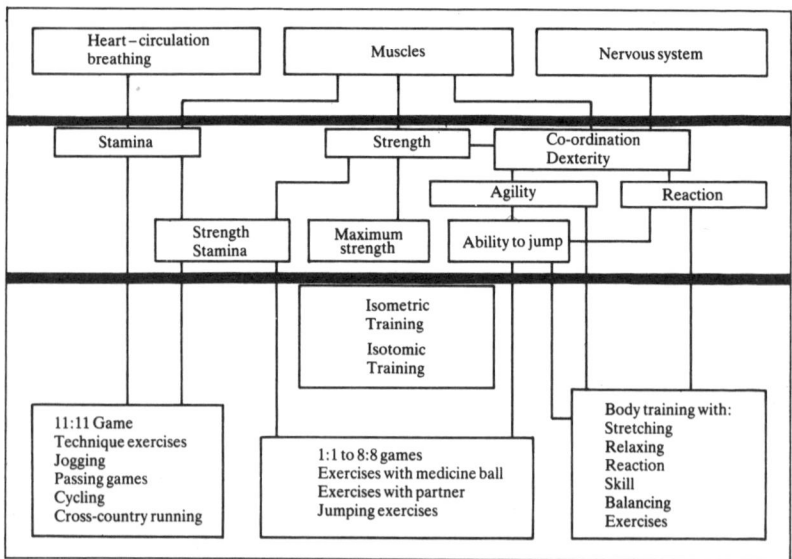

Fitness and condition

How to lead your life dedicated to sport

To achieve proper fitness and condition, value must be put on a complete sporting way of life as well as on sports training. The diagram below shows what should be given proper attention. If your way of life includes playing a sport, you will be substantially more efficient in your sport and in your job compared with people of the same age who may have the talent but lack the training.

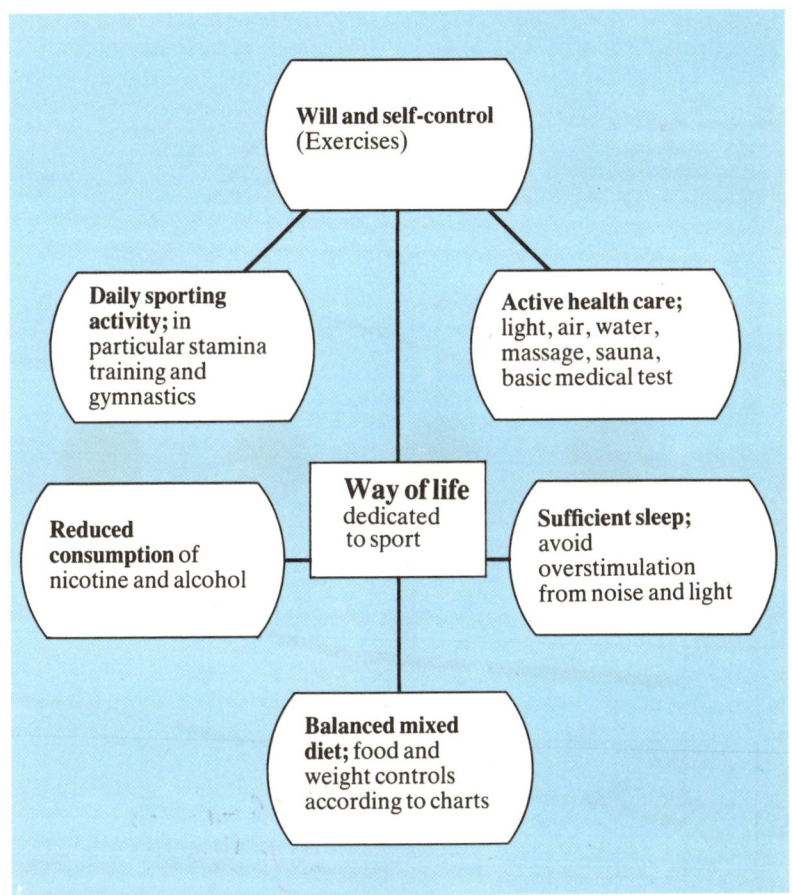

Fitness and condition

Fitness and daily exercise

An organism that has been made fit through daily sporting activity and a way of life dedicated to sport is in a far better position to cope with everyday physical, mental and emotional strain.

Primarily it is the positive effect of sport on the heart-circulatory system that keeps the sportsman functioning properly and young in the truest sense of the word. According to the opinions of many important scientists, there are even today no medicines or preparations that could replace sport.

The two following charts clearly show to what additional strain the heart and circulation of people whose bodies have not been made efficient through sports training are exposed.

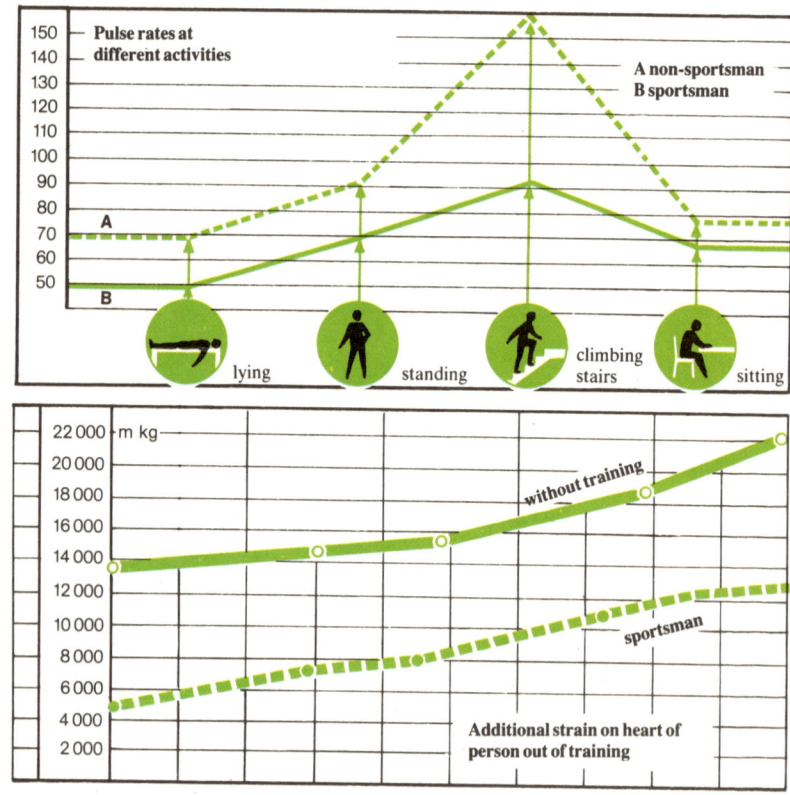

Fitness and condition

Fitness and condition

The circulatory system of a person in training works smoothly and calmly, so that his heart has a substantially smaller amount of work to do per day than that of a person not in training.

The basics of training

There is a method of training to suit every aspect of bodily fitness (see diagram on page 58).

Today there is no general condition training any more. Methods of improving, for example, stamina and the ability to jump are as different as the special training for the instep kick and running off the ball. It is therefore worth choosing the exercises for condition training systematically and specifically. Likewise the duration of the exercises and the pauses between them must be fixed according to the individual.

During the course of a training session only two aspects of bodily fitness should be concentrated on at the same time. As an example, stamina training and speed training basically exclude one another.

There is one optimum training method for every aspect of bodily activity. The training methods are decided by the following:

- Intensity of the exercise
  This depends on the energy consumed in an exercise and the speed with which a certain distance or a given exercise is completed. Intensity is designated as maximum, strong, medium and moderate; it can also be expressed in percentages of maximum achievement (=%).
- Extent of the exercise
  This is reckoned on the number of times the exercise is repeated, running distances covered or the time in which the exercises and games are performed.
- Duration of the exercise
- Breaks between exercises
  The duration of the exercise and the breaks in between depend very heavily on the intensity and the extent of the exercises. These, for their part, are determined once again by the choice of exercises, games and competitions. Highly intensive training must, as a rule, be limited. The duration of the individual exercise is relatively short and likewise the breaks in between, ie the pauses between the intensive exercises should be longer. In the case of exercising several parts of the body at the same time, the overall effect is less intense.

Training methods

From the way in which the intensity, extent, duration and breaks between the exercises combine with one another, definite training methods result. Today there are essentially four different methods of which only three are important for soccer fitness and condition training:

- the sustained achievement method
- the extensive interval method
- the intensive interval method

The repetition method, in which highly intensive exercises are selected, originates from body-building. It is not suitable either for general fitness or for specific soccer condition training.

The adjacent table shows which training methods improve certain aspects of bodily fitness. Suitable training means (ie exercises, games, etc) are given for the methods in each case. The ratio of intensity, extent, duration and breaks in between exercises are listed in the last three columns. Each person can draw up his own fitness schedule and his specific condition training with the help of this table. It is a great help if an exercise and training plan can be prepared some weeks in advance.

Training methods	Training aims/motivation
1 Sustained achievement method	Long-term stamina General & special basic stamina Improved capacity for oxygen intake through improvement of heart–circulation–breathing–achievement
2 Extensive interval method	Middle-term stamina 2-8min
3 Intensive interval method	Short-term duration– 45-120sec. Speed stamina Ability to jump in two-man tests etc. Initial speed Leg power Kicking power

Fitness and condition

Means of training (examples)	Intensity of exercise	Extent/Duration of exercise	Arrangement of pauses
Runs: Forest run, passing games, runs with tempo changes **Games:** 3:1, 4:2, 8:8 to 11:11 **Ball work:** On the move	**Runs:** Moderate-middle 40%-50% **Games:** 6:6 with ¼-sized pitch and small goals **Weights:** 25%-40%	**Runs:** 5000m/Seniors 3000m/Juniors 2000m/School children **Games:** At least 30min **Ball work:** At least 45min	No passive breaks Only change in intensity or type of exercise
Runs: Runs with tempo changes Runs up slopes Runs up hills **Games:** 3:3+3, 3:3 to 6:6 **Ball work:** On the move with opponent with breaks (change in task)	**Runs:** Middle-fast 60%-70% **Games:** 3:3+3, 3:3 to 6:6 on ¼ to ½-sized pitch **Ball work:** At fast running tempo **Weights:** 40%-60%	**Runs:** 3-5 series of 4-10 runs over 20-200m **Games:** 3:5 games from 90-180 sec **Ball work:** Complex exercises 3-5 exercises to 4-10 repeats	Active breaks with gymnastics, exercises in technique; feel pulse down to 140 Length of breaks: 1-2 min
Runs: Starts from standing, sitting, lying Exercises with partner **Games:** 1:1, 2:2, 1:2, 2:1, 3:3 **Ball work:** With weighted vest; with opponent	**Runs:** Fast-sub max 80-90% **Games:** 1:1, 2:2, 1:2, 3:3 at top running tempo **Ball work:** Max use **Weights:** 50-75%	**Runs:** 4-6 series of 2-5 starts over 10-70m **Games:** 5-10 games at 30-60sec **Ball work:** Complex exercises 4-6 exercises with 2-5 repeats	Alternately active and passive breaks, ie pulse at 120 or reduced to 80, approx. 2-4min Break between series

Training plans

People who want to slim or would like to undertake sports training should, as far as possible, be active daily. Usually it is sufficient if a sportsman undergoes intensive training twice a week, for example in a club. On the other days of the week he can keep up and improve his physical fitness by taking short runs in the woods or jogging, by early morning gymnastics or swimming or visits to the sauna.

It is important, however, that the fitness régime should be planned carefully. Therefore, you should draw up a training plan starting from your present capabilities. If the plan is written down, it not only gives a better overall view, but also helps you to vary the routine. Not least, a written training plan also encourages you to be active on the days when you would rather be lazy.

The training plan should be drawn up in such a way that first stamina, then strength and lastly speed are practised. Gymnastic exercises to improve flexibility can be interspersed in each single training unit.

Example of a 4-week training plan.

	Training Aim
1st Week	
Monday	Stamina
Tuesday	Loosening up
Wednesday	Regeneration
Thursday	Technique, agility
Friday	Stamina, loosening up, technique
Sat/Sun	Game
2nd Week	
Monday	Relaxation
Tuesday	Technique, strength
Wednesday	Medium stamina
Thursday	Technique, tactics
Friday	Loosening up
Sat/Sun	Game
3rd Week	
Monday	Relaxation
Tuesday	Technique, speed
Wednesday	Training game
Thursday	Technique, loosening up
Friday	Stretching
Sat/Sun	Game
4th Week	
Monday	Loosening up, regenerati
Tuesday	Medium stamina
Wednesday	—
Thursday	Technique, tactics
Friday	Ball work
Sat/Sun	Game

Fitness and condition

The training plan below for an active player allows for a daily exercise period in a club (C) or at home (H). The training plan should be carried out straight away; don't waste any more time.

Means of Training	Training Method	Duration	Place
Cross-country running	Sustained Method	20-30 min.	H
Gymnastics with ball	Sustained Method	10 min.	H
Swimming	Interval Method	45 min.	H
Training	—	90 min.	C
Individual work with ball	Interval Method	20-30 min.	H
Match	—	90 min.	C
Sauna+Gymnastics	—	60 min.	H
Training	—	90 min.	C
Running with tempo changes	Extensive Int. Method	30 min.	H
Training	—	90 min.	C
Gymnastics with ball	Sustained Method	20 min.	H
Match	—	90 min.	C
Sauna+Swimming	—	90 min.	H
Training	—	60 min.	C
Match	—	90 min.	C
Training	—	60 min.	C
Gymnastics	Sustained Method	15 min.	H
Match	—	90 min.	C
Running in woods, running	Moderate runs with breaks	45 min.	H
Training	—	90 min.	C
—	—		
Training	—	90 min.	C
Gymnastics	any	30 min.	H
Match	—	90 min.	C

Training means

The term 'training means' includes exercises, methods of play and matches, all of which go to make up training.

The setting-up of training means can be carried out in at least two ways. Different means of training are suitable according to whether you train alone, with a partner, with a group of players at a similar level to your own or within the family.

A further difference arises out of the training target you have set yourself. The tables on pages 62 and 63 give a good idea of this. A series of further examples are set out on pages 67-73.

Together with the training guidelines that are mentioned in the special techniques, it must be possible for everyone who has read this book to draw up an individual, varied training plan for himself or for others. You must not underestimate your mental attitude to training. It should basically be a happy one, but should be serious as well. Physical reserves can be called upon only if you have the will to get the most out of your training.

Running

Basic stamina
Run in woods: 3-6km at a speed where the pulse settles down to a

Areas for fitness training within the family unit can be found everywhere. Here a father and daughter are taking penalty kicks, the son is going round slalom poles, while the mother keeps fit by exercising with a ball.

Fitness and condition

rate of approximately 180 less your age (for example, 160 if you are 20).

The following training plan is recommended:

Frequency	Distance of run	Running time in exercise period
1-9 weeks 5 x per week	each 1.5km	13.30 max 9.15 min
from 10 weeks 2 x per week	each 1.5km	9.00 max 7.45 min
	each 2.5km	16.00 max 11.55 min
	each 3.0km	to 17.00 min

Stamina at speed
Running up slopes and changes in speed with and without a ball, gymnastic exercises in between, also runs at a set pace around slalom poles, jumping over hurdles and so on – for example, 12-15 times 100m in 14-16 seconds with 60-90 seconds break in each case; or 10 times 200m in 32-36 seconds with 90-120 seconds break in each case.

Ability to jump
Running up steps and hills at full strength until thigh muscles are totally exhausted; trot slowly downhill, then break until pulse is down once again to 80.

Training means

Relays and races

Pendulum relay
Three players to each relay: two players are on one touchline with the ball, the third is opposite them on the other touchline. When the whistle blows, the first player runs across the field and hands or passes the ball to the waiting player who kicks it back to the third man. Three to five runs per man, then break.

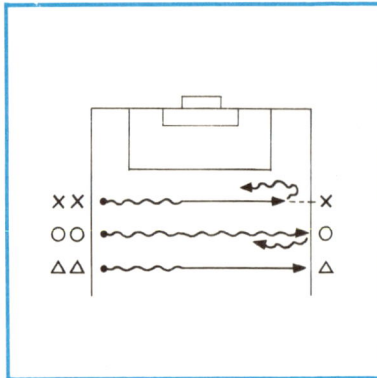

Pursuit race round the 18-yard area
All relays are positioned at one corner of the 18-yard area with a ball each. Relay A of the first group runs, with B and C at a distance of about 2m each behind. Each kicks the ball round the 18-yard area as quickly as possible and hands it after one circuit to the second runner. Each group tries to overtake those in front or shake off those behind.

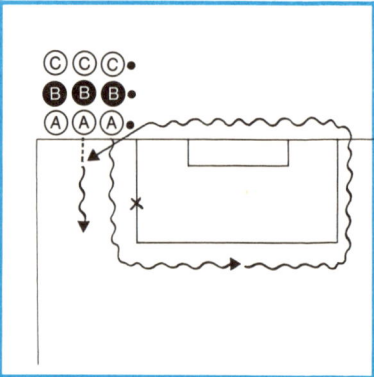

Diagonal runs
There are four players at each corner of half the pitch. The first player of each group has a ball. When called, the four players run diagonally across to the opposite corner. A change of pace will avoid collisions in the middle of the area.

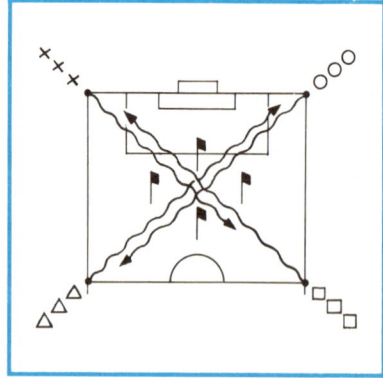

Fitness and condition

Types of games – individual activity

Keeping the ball in the air
According to your level of ability, the ball should only bounce once or not at all. Better players keep the ball in the air while moving forwards.

Rocket-launching
Hit the ball straight up in the air as high as possible and stop it the moment it touches the ground or volley it.

Ball over the rope
Play the ball over a taut rope at above head height – or over a bush; then run round to the other side. The ball should not touch the ground more than twice, better only once, on each side.

Ball acrobatics
Once again hit the ball as high as possible and immediately do a press-up, a forwards or backwards roll or a kangaroo jump before catching or stopping the ball the moment it touches the ground.

Note: Technique and form (special speed and co-ordination) are also improved using the types of games described here.

Training means

Types of games with a partner

One against one
On an area that has been marked out, play either without goals or towards one or two goals. Maximum playing time is two minutes, due to high intensity. Then take an active break; play 'keeping the ball in the air', for example, during the break.

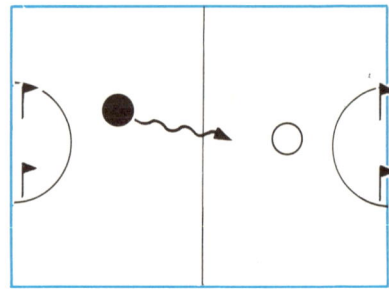

Soccer tennis
Play on a marked-out area over a rope at hip-to-head height. Two, one or no ball contacts with the ground, according to your level of skill. Technique as preferred.

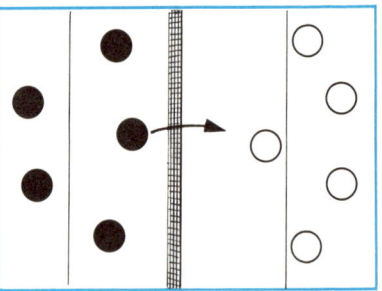

Drive ball game
On an area of about 20 x 100 metres, the opponent is driven back into his own area by playing the ball as far from him as possible with instep kicks. Opponent kicks the ball back again from the place where he retrieved it or where it touched the ground.

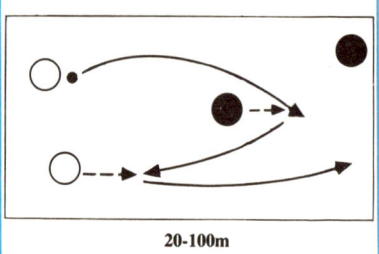

20-100m

Practising shots
In a marked-out area, player A tries to hit player B with shots in the air or along the ground. Every time he hits, he scores a point. Change roles after two minutes. This game is particularly suitable for a gymnasium.

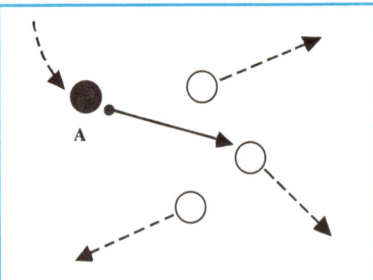

Fitness and condition

Team games

Two against one
On a marked-out pitch, two players pass the ball to each other so that a third player cannot get to it. Passing either direct or, as preferred, after dribbling. It is possible to play the 'two against one' game at goal.

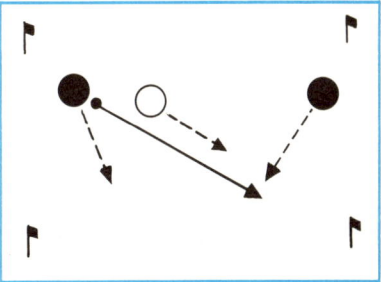

Tag
Up to eight players stand in a circle and pass the ball directly to one another so that the 'chasers' (up to four) in the middle cannot get to the ball.

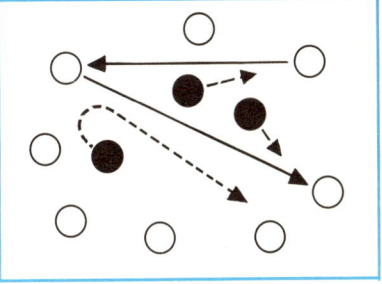

Three against three alternately with three teams
Team A attacks first, challenged by team B. When B wins the ball it is then challenged by C. The game can be played at goal or over the line. In the latter case, a point is scored when the ball is dribbled over the line.

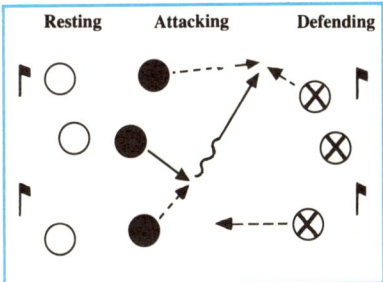

Game with two neutral players
Two to eight players can play in each team. Two neutral players stand at either end of the pitch; each pass to a neutral player scores a point. Passes can be scored either alternately with each neutral player or at random.

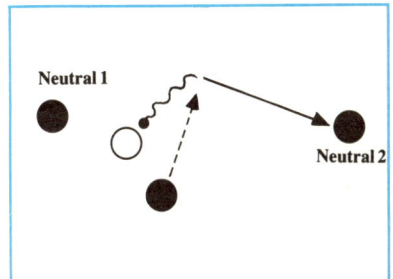

Training means

Circuit training

Circuit training is a modern system to improve fitness. Different practice or game stages are arranged in a circuit one after the other.

The circuit opposite is made of technique and fitness exercises. A medicine ball is used instead of a football to intensify the exercises.

In a technique and fitness circuit the exercise period at each stage is between 20 and 60 seconds. The player must repeat the exercises as many times as possible within this period.

You can also set yourself a specific number of times per stage the exercise has to be carried out and then make yourself – or anyone else – go round the entire circuit in the shortest possible time. If concentrated technique exercises or small games, for example 'two against one' or 'one against one' are included at the exercise stages, tactics can also be improved as well as technique and fitness.

In technique, fitness and tactical circuits, the exercise periods at each stage should be between one and three minutes. The longer exercise or game time at each stage is necessary because some games require a certain run-up time and the practice effect is only felt after a minimum period.

Improvement in general and specific fitness

1 Jumping practice
2 Body and arm strengthening
3 Improving shooting power
4 Leg, body and arm strengthening
5 Strengthening stomach muscles
6 Jumping stamina
7 Strengthening shoulders and body
8 Toughening back muscles

Each exercise 10-30 times according to maximum effect required

Tactics

Tactics make up the third factor of good play after technique and fitness. The aim of soccer tactics is quite simple: 'to score goals, prevent goals being scored against you and beat your opponent by skilful, correct use of technique and fitness qualities. The following factors in tactics must be taken into account:
- your own capabilities
- the opponent with all his qualities and capabilities
- the opponent's tactical plan
- the present state of the game
- the play situation
- the weather, ground conditions, pitch size, etc.

To use tactics properly, a player must watch his opponent and the play situation closely, weigh up different possibilities and then plan and act quickly on the basis of his tactical experience and knowledge.

A player needs the following requirements:
- he must watch the run of play very carefully
- he must know how to cope successfully with certain situations in play
- he must be in a situation to put the tactical plan into action quickly, decisively and independently.

The significance of tactics in play performance

If we are to believe what we are told by managers, tactics – which the manager has worked out in the privacy of his own room – are directly responsible for the result of a game. Since managers very seldom blame their own tactics after their team has been beaten, however, the great importance attached to tactics for the results of a game must be challenged. This is certainly true as long as tactics are thought to be only a concoction of brilliant ideas thought up by the manager.

However tactics are in fact much simpler than the acrobatic chess game suggested. Soccer is basically a simple game in which certain standard situations crop up regularly; it ends up again and again as a contest between attacker and defender. In every game there are a number of situations of play governed by rules such as corners, free kicks, etc. Certain possible solutions have emerged in practice as being particularly effective and successful for all these standard situations. Helmut Schön, the famous West German coach, often pointed out that the training of players depends initially on teaching this basic understanding of tactics.

Team tactics
Offensive game – Defensive game
Playing for time – Keeping the ball
Teamwork between groups

Attacking tactics
Running off the ball
Making concerted moves
Position changing
Breakthrough
Dribbling
Goal shot
Play in centre forward position
Play on the wing
Counter-attack
Position attack
Standard situations (corner, free kick etc.)

Soccer – tactics

Defensive tactics
Positional play
Marking man or ground
Tackling
Marking as a team
Protecting
Surrendering – taking over
Offside trap
Teamwork with goalkeeper
Teamwork with sweeper
Standard situations (corner, free kick etc.)

General individual tactics
Get to the man with the ball!
Run towards the ball!
Don't let any ball bounce!
Don't let any ball past!
Body between man and ball!

Tactical play positions with the 4:3:3 system
Goalkeeper, full-backs and central defender, sweeper
3 midfield players
Wings and centre forward

Special tactics dependent on opponent, state of play, weather etc.
standard situations governed by rules (kick-off, free kick, corner, thrown-in)

Tactics

Marking and running off the ball

Soccer reaches its high point as a competitive sport with dribbling, tackling, marking and running off the ball. The defender is constantly occupied in preventing his opposite number getting to the ball or shooting at goal. On the other hand, the striker uses all possible means to escape his marker. Proper running off the ball is one of the most important aspects of tactical play. By skilful running off the ball you can:

- escape from your opponent's marking
- create a chance to pass to a team-mate
- provide an opening for a team-mate to break through
- change positions with a team-mate.

The series of photographs opposite shows how to run off the ball correctly.

The striker is blocked by close marking, but suddenly breaks forward at great speed when his team-mate catches his eye to show that he is ready to pass. To shake off his opponent, who is pursuing him, the striker suddenly checks and runs towards the team-mate who wants to pass him the ball, so that when it is passed he is free and can receive the ball unchallenged – for a moment or two, anyway.

Marking

When forwards used to outnumber defenders, the defenders generaly stood between two attackers and blocked them by marking the ground. Until the Sixties, this was the case with the 'WM' system. When the 4-4-2 and 4-3-3 systems were introduced, the numbers balanced out, even producing numerical superiority in defence. The defenders could now afford to shadow their opposite numbers by marking them directly. Players particularly good at technique – and the creative players in the team – were blocked by excellent, very close marking.

When marking a man, the following points should be borne in mind:

- the defender stands between his opponent and his own goal
- he always keeps his opponent and the ball in sight
- he marks on the side closest to the ball, at an angle behind the opponent.

Lately the forwards have learnt to get round even this tough marking with their increasing finesse and particularly through a tactically skilful mixture of the 'one-two' pass and dribbling.

Even the sweeper, positioned behind the defenders marking their men, is seldom in a position to close all the gaps by marking the ground. In the 4-3-3 system, incidentally, this is known as mixed marking.

Teams are now reverting to ground marking. Here each player is assigned a certain area for which he is responsible. Any striker who penetrates this area is picked up by the relevant defending player. Modern method teams build up at least three flexible chains of defence in front of goal. According to experience, the opposing strikers are caught in this defence net sooner than if they had only to face man-for-man marking.

A particular difficulty with this type of ground marking is the fact that several defenders must work hand in hand to a certain extent. If just one player fails, for example through bad form on the day or through a slack piece of play, the defence net can very easily be broken further. One particular advantage of this type of marking is that midfield players and strikers can change positions with defenders; in this way the switch from defence to attack can be carried out very quickly and smoothly.

Tactics

Forms of training

Marking and running off the ball can be done using the following exercises and games:

One plus one against one
The striker tries to shake off his defender with a quick burst of speed so that his team-mate can pass to him. The player passing the ball can also serve several pairs of strikers and defenders.

Game with three against one or four against two
In a marked-out pitch of about 20 x 20 metres: for the striker, 'get the man with the ball' is a good rule. The defending players must operate using ground marking because the strikers are superior in numbers.

Roll ball, handball or basketball in square groups with two goals or baskets
The ball should not be kicked above head height since the strikers must run free into the path of the ball. The defending player either marks his man or marks the ground.

Game with five against five up to ten against ten into one goal
The rapid switch from attack to defence and thus from free running to marking is better used with this game. If the attacking team loses the ball, each player must switch to marking the ground or his man as per instructions.

Systems of play

Each individual in the team is assigned his position, territory and task. One system of play is not necessarily suited to every team, so the system that a team uses should be geared more to the individual types of player within the team. Modern systems of play safeguard the area in front of goal very well; however, at the same time attacking play forces not only the strikers but also the defenders forward into the fray alternately.

The two most popular systems of play today are the so-called 4-3-3 system and, as a variation, the 4-4-2 system.

The system itself only represents the outer framework, however. According to the types of player available and the tactical method, it can be played with a number of variations.

While the system of play normally gives rise to the tactics to be deployed, in special cases it can be varied for a short period for tactical reasons. For example, when a team that has begun with the defensive 4-4-2 system finds itself a goal down towards the end of a game, it will have to switch for tactical reasons to the more attacking 4-3-3 system.

The 4-3-3 system

The 10 outfield players form themselves into three groups. The defence consists of a sweeper covering the defence, two full-backs and one central defender; the midfield is formed by one defensive, one central and one attacking midfield player; the attack consists of the outside right, the outside left and the centre forward.

Should the team find itself on the defensive, at least each of the three midfield players pulls back into a defending position, frequently with the forwards, too. In this way they form another defence mechanism – mostly by marking an area of ground – in front of the defenders who are marking their men. If the team is on the attack, a midfield player moves into the opponents' half of the field along with the three spearhead forwards.

The 4-4-2 system

Teams that use the 4-4-2 system operate even more defensively. A man is pulled back from the three spearhead forwards to reinforce the midfield. The two strikers left are positioned in the midle in front of the opponents' goal and thus deliberately leave both wings free. Either midfield or defensive players make runs upfield into these free areas.

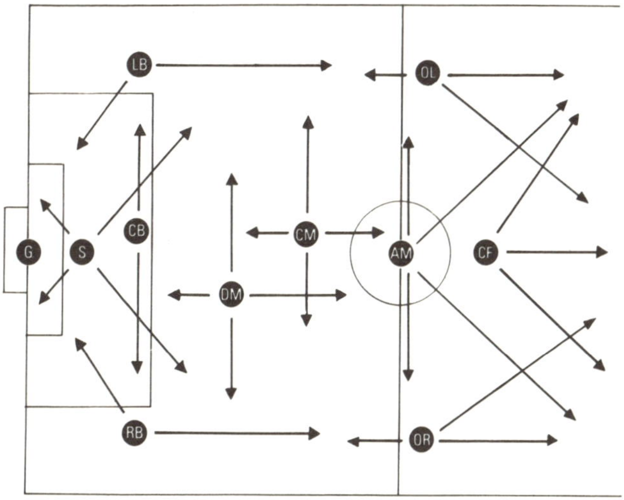

Tactics

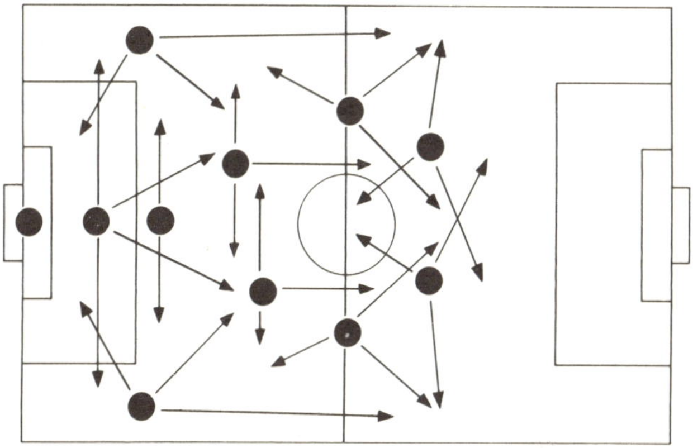

Team positions

Goalkeeper
The goalkeeper's main task in co-operation with his defenders is to prevent the opponents scoring goals. His job in detail amounts to the following;
- to marshal the defence
- to save shots at goal
- to catch crosses and other passes in the 18-yard area
- to block players who have broken through by running out of goal at the right time, thus reducing the angle of the shot.

Moreover the goalkeeper is primarily the one who launches an attack and who must decide at lightning speed whether a new attack should be started quickly with a throw-out or by kicking upfield as far as possible. He should always bear in mind whether a move should be made quickly or whether play should be slowed down within the rules.

Sweeper
In all modern systems of play, behind the last line of defence there is the so-called free man who does not have an immediate marking task, but has to move quickly to any danger area. The sweeper is a typical product of modern systems of play. The following tasks are given to him:
- setting up the defence
- covering the players in front of him
- blocking any opposing forwards who have broken through, about 25 metres from the goal
- starting counter-attacks with accurate passes
- going on the offensive himself and supporting his team's attack

Full-backs and central defenders
They normally mark their opposite numbers. Only the full-back goes back to marking the ground – moving in towards the goal – when the game is not being played on his side of the field.

One of the full-back's important tasks is to push forward suddenly into the opposing team's half of the field and to add weight to the attack. The defenders' forward thrusts should basically end up with a shot at goal, a cross or a safe pass. Any risky dribbling should be avoided.

Midfield players
The three midfield players in the 4-3-3 system or the four players in the 4-4-2 system have, as their main task, to fluctuate between attack and defence. If an opponent has the ball, they pull back completely and reinforce their own defence; if their own team has the ball, they have the following offensive tasks:
- to help the spearhead forwards with accurate passes

Tactics

- to be available for return and 'one-two' passes
- to push forward in turn into the forefront of the attack
- to take a sudden shot at goal from behind the main line of attack.

Spearhead forwards
Since they have to battle against large numbers of defenders, they must be pure attack specialists and master completely the following means of attack:
- shots at goal using feet and head
- breaking through and dribbling
- widening and deepening their positions when necessary
- all types of teamwork, such as the 'one-two' and similar movements.

Special training

In addition to the general training plan, each player should include exercises in his training plan that are related to his position.

Goalkeeper
The technical aspects such as catching, fisting and diving are worked on generally in individual training alongside the specific qualities of fitness such as flexibility, co-ordination, nimbleness and leg power.

Tactical skills such as reducing angles, running out on the correct side, teamwork with defenders and so on are developed together with defenders and forwards according to modern methods of play.

Defenders
In particular defenders must work on the technique of winning the ball, heading and volleying. This is best done through individual exercises in which the player learns to check another, first by dummy attacks and then by real attacks. Great speed, quick reactions, agility and strength in a challenge are especially important for the defender. These qualities can be improved partly by individual running, but are better done through challenges between two players and mini-games such as 'one against one', etc. At the same time, this gives experience in tactically correct defensive play – that is, proper marking and tackling.

WESTERN RESERVE HIGH SCHOOL
LIBRARY

Playing groups

Midfield players
Receiving the ball cleanly and moving off with it while running and turning, as well as accurate passing over short and long distances, are the main tasks midfield players should work on. They should also perfect shooting while on the run from distances between 16 and 25 metres.

They must be trained tactically as forwards and defenders. They must learn to shift the game from one half of the field to the other and change positions with team-mates in the spearhead.
As far as fitness is concerned, midfield players should develop all aspects of stamina so that even in the 89th minute they can still get the better of their opponents.

Spearhead forwards
Dribbling and feinting, quick passing of the ball, centering and scoring goals with either foot, or the head, from long or short distances – the spearhead forwards must repeat all these tirelessly. Bursts towards goal, the goal-hunting instinct, firm decision-making and challenging, as well as speed, can be employed and improved in mini-games towards a single objective. Individual and group action that is tactically correct can be combined with fitness in complex exercises and games. Sudden bursts of speed should be used intensively by forwards.

Playing groups

Attackers
As will be shown below, attacking players primarily have to solve a number of differing tactical problems as forwards. It must be pointed out, nevertheless, that they are the first defenders in their own team when an opposing defender has the ball. Every forward has to put his opposite number under pressure with accurate passing and immediately pursue him whenever the latter moves forward into the attack. The forward's attacking play is built up either close to the touchline as wing play or in the middle of the field in front of the opponent's goal.

Play on the wing
A wing forward and a midfield player always participate in this – and frequently the centre forward, too. The aim of wing play is to draw the opponents' defence, in particular the sweeper, away from goal and thereby create free areas and therefore good shooting possibilities for their own advancing midfield players and the other wing forward.

Tactics

Play in the centre forward position

Play here is particularly difficult because the sweeper additionally marks the area in front of goal. Against this reinforced bastion of defence, the forwards use the following moves:
- the sweeper is compelled to leave his position in front of goal by the wing play previously described
- the front midfield player penetrates right into the front line as a second centre forward and thereby ties down the sweeper
- as long as the ball is not nearby, the centre forward moves towards the sweeper, thereby tying down his immediate opponent, who is marking him, and the sweeper in a restricted area at the same time
- the static defence structure is broken down briefly if two or three strikers change positions across and up the field
- various types of play using the defensive wall and the 'one-two' overcome mixed marking of players and areas.

Defensive players

We have already talked about teamwork and defensive players in the preceding pages. For example, we mentioned that the sweeper (marking an area) and the defenders (marking their man) produce a type of mixed marking – more recently just ground marking. It is, perhaps, best described as 'marking the man in the area'. In this way every player involved in defence is assigned a certain territory to defend. Any opponent who penetrates into this area is taken on by the defender responsible for marking it; the nearer the opponent approaches to goal, the closer he is marked.

With this method of marking, teamwork and co-operation between defenders is absolutely vital. Two tactical moves characterise this type of defence:
- covering a team-mate
- handing over an opponent

To protect a defender fighting off an opponent, the area of ground is covered either by the sweeper or the other full-back advancing infield. The covering player positions himself at an angle about 3 metres behind the defender to protect the open side.

If the challenging defender is beaten by the striker, the second tactical move is made. The striker is challenged by the covering defender to slow him down; the other defender, who was beaten off, immediately runs back and takes over covering the second defender.

Special situations in the game

Soccer is an uncomplicated game in which certain situations occur again and again. Fans find this an especially fascinating aspect of the game, since they anticipate the development of a play situation and then wait to see how the players try to solve it.

There are a number of proved possible solutions for situations of play, such as the free kick, the corner, the kick-off and the throw-in. According to the special technical skills of its players and of the opponents, a team should opt for different tactical moves. For example, you should always kick a corner against a hesitant goalkeeper and to forwards who are good at heading in front of goal in such a way that the corresponding weaknesses and strengths are brought into play.

Free kick

Around the penalty area, you should try to score directly off free kicks. If this is not possible, a free kick can be used indirectly according to one of the two variations below.

Lobbed free kick

One player suddenly lobs the ball to a team-mate positioned in front of the wall, who then passes it over the wall to a striker who has started his run towards goal.

Sideways pass around the wall

Two or three players gather together near the ball. One or two players start to run past the wall, either straight past it or across it. One takes the pass on the run and tries to get past the wall and let go a shot at goal.

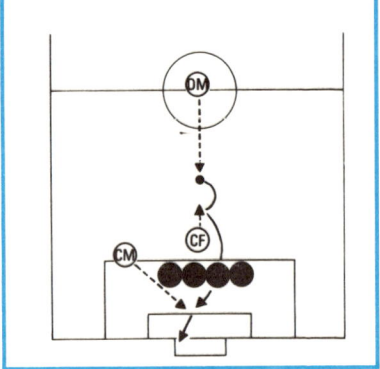

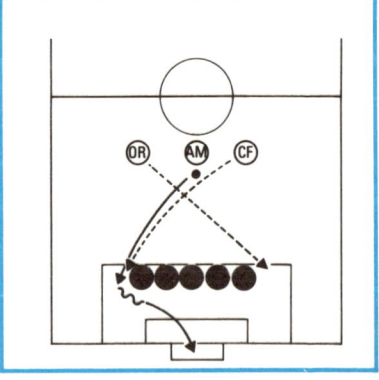

Tactics

Corner kick

Ground variations are classified as follows:

- the short corner kick over 3 to 10 metres to a team-mate running out
- the semi-high corner to the near post
- the high corner that curls in towards goal or bends away from it
- the corner that is pulled back to the edge of the penalty area for a player in space to have a shot at goal.

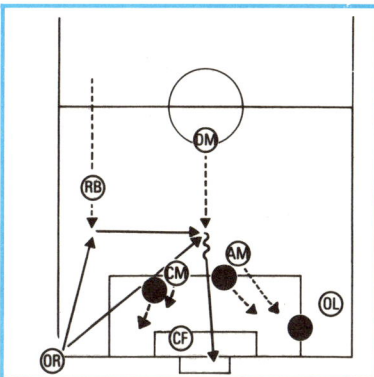

Semi-high corner

If the opponents have superior heading techniques, a player runs towards the semi-high corner when called. There are several possibilities open to him:

- shooting directly at goal
- playing the ball back to his own players
- passing it back again to the player who took the corner.

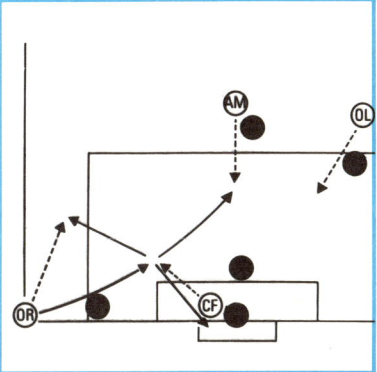

High corner

If there are heading specialists in your own team, curl this corner in to the far post or away from the goal into an area that has deliberately been kept free of strikers. At the moment the corner is taken, several of your team who are good at heading start running into this space to score.

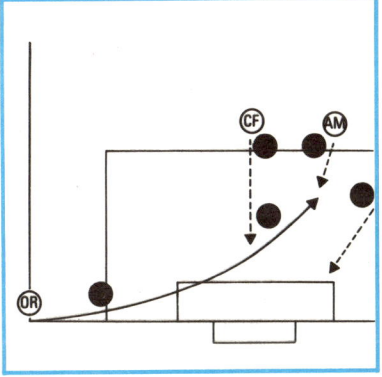

Tactics on the day

With every game there are different conditions to which a team should adjust itself tactically:
- external circumstances such as the weather, ground conditions, position of the sun and the proportions of the pitch
- the opponents' qualities of technique, fitness and tactics
- home or away game.

External circumstances

Shortly before the game, the condition of the pitch and environmental factors should be checked by going out to inspect the pitch.

Pitch size

The size of a pitch can vary between 90 and 120 metres in length and 45 and 90 metres in width. The regulations only state that the pitch must be longer than it is wide. The pitch can therefore be extremely small or large, almost square or tube-like. On large pitches strong, fit players are used to chasing across the field after long balls. Agile players good at technique feel more at home on small pitches. These points should be considered when choosing players to make up a team for individual matches.

Ground conditions

On wet, slippery and icy surfaces, it is best to use safe, short, accurate passes to your team-mates' feet. The man with the ball tries to wear down defenders by dribbling and feinting. Shots from all positions – including the second line of attack – are likely to succeed. When the ground is very muddy or covered in snow, an uncomplicated 'kick-and-rush' game using a lot of space is often preferable.

Air temperature

When it is very hot, experienced players frequently take salt tablets to compensate for salt loss, which otherwise leads to cramp. Those looking after the players, the trainers, keep refreshing drinks ready and special liniment to cool the neck and chest. Conversely, in extreme cold, protective tights, gloves and headbands are recommended.

Position of sun and direction of wind

In the second half, as evening draws on, the sun can disappear behind trees, houses, stands and so on; also the wind can change, increasing or dropping. Managers and trainers should try to gain a tactical advantage from general conditions such as these.

Tactics

How the opposition play

Tactics on the day, both for the individual player and for the whole team, depend very much on the ability of the opposition:
- physical capabilities
- technical skill
- tactical method

An opponent's fitness determines his own method of play. You should never play offensively against a player who is physically fitter than yourself. Since his superior strength will tell the more the game goes on, your comparative weakness would be an embarrassment. It is therefore more effective to chase your opponent round, marking him even more closely, using technical means such as holding on to the ball intelligently and changing the wings, until his physical superiority is exhausted. Strength-sapping dribbling and through balls into open space should be avoided. Of course, the ball should be kept low against a particularly tall opponent. When your opponent's technique is superior, but you are convinced your physical condition is better than his, then patience and strong nerves should be your tactics.

In spite of occasional technical mistakes in their own ranks and the opponents' apparent superiority, fit teams should not give up. Their time often only comes in the last 15-30 minutes of the game. Until then they must chase the opponents about all over the pitch according to all the rules of tactical play. If the opponent has the ball then, wherever possible, all your players should pull back in front of goal to entice the opposing team out of its half. If you gain possession of the ball, push your opponents back down the whole pitch using long, wide-reaching counter-attacks. This constant running to and fro will soon tire out less fit opponents.

In this connection it should also be pointed out that the 'man against man' tussle is not only carried out using technical and tactical means and physical fitness. Particularly cunning players give their time and attention to the psychological strengths and weaknesses of their opponents. In this way sensitive types of players very often have their playing rhythm destroyed early on by hard, but fair, challenges; equally you can try to get a particularly hard opponent to play somewhat more carefully by a 'friendly' word on the side.

Sporting injuries

Injuries – avoidance and treatment

As in every sporting activity, there is a certain risk of injury in games of soccer, in particular in the two-man exchanges which make this sport so attractive.

According to statistics, in relation to the number of people who play the sport, soccer sits at the top of the dangerous sports table – with 3.2% injuries.

Legs, body, shoulders and head are often injured in various ways. The danger of injury cannot be removed completely, but it can certainly be reduced by taking preventative measures:

1. A healthy way of life, sufficient sleep, care of the body, baths, massage and saunas
2. Regular training
3. Prompt treatment of ailments – for example, tooth extraction or removing infected tonsils
4. After illnesses and injuries build yourself up carefully
5. Observe the principles of training; for example, alternate between work and relaxation, correct strength build-up
6. Warming up and loosening up: warm up for at least 15 minutes before a match with gymnastic stretching exercises

Sporting injuries

Types of injury

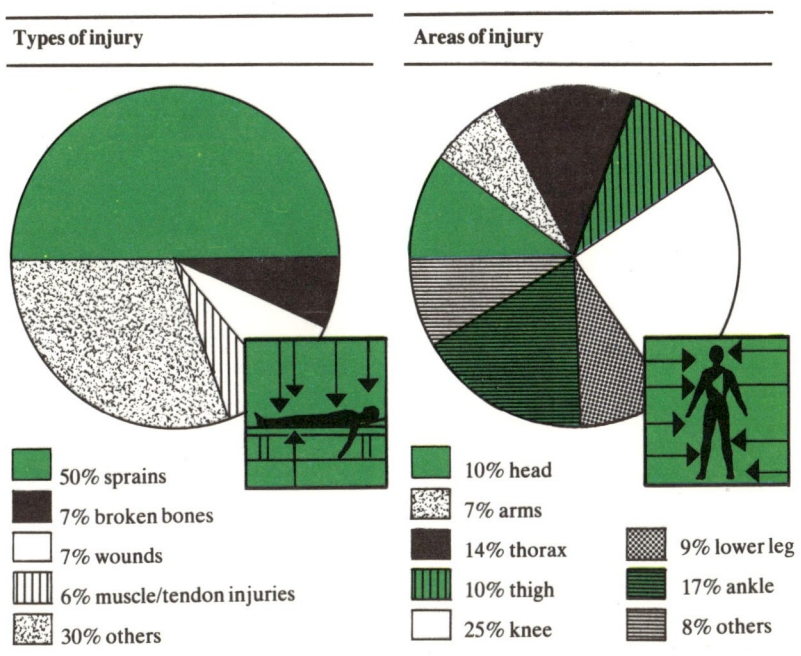

- 50% sprains
- 7% broken bones
- 7% wounds
- 6% muscle/tendon injuries
- 30% others

Areas of injury

- 10% head
- 7% arms
- 14% thorax
- 10% thigh
- 25% knee
- 9% lower leg
- 17% ankle
- 8% others

7 Always use shin guards and bandages if necessary
8 Avoid using creams that inflame the skin
9 Tendency towards muscle cramp; take salt tablets.

Methods of treatment

If, in spite of observing the above-mentioned preventative measures, a player sustains an injury, there are a number of possible treatments. In this connection there is a difference to be made between initial treatment, which can be carried out as quickly and expertly as possible by the player himself or by a trainer, and the further treatment, which is given by a doctor or physiotherapist.

Methods of treatment

The initial treatment is of great importance if the injury is to heal quickly and successfully. The healing process, ie the time in which a player is out of the game, can be reduced to half the usual treatment time by expert initial attention. During the further treatment, too, the patient should actively benefit from individual treatment. To this end some basic knowledge of the types of injury and their treatment are important. Therefore on these next pages methods of treatment are described briefly.

Ice and cold treatment
Cold treatment is the most important of all the possible initial measures. The chlorethyl cold spray is part of every trainer's standard equipment. Unfortunately, when it is used after pulling ligaments or muscles, sprains or muscle bruising as a means of reducing pain through cold shock, it does not prevent a bruise from forming – unless subsequent ice treatment is applied. The bruise and the germs and bacteria that form around the damaged tissue are what often prolong injuries.

Both bruises and harmful tissue germs can be reduced to a minimum if you rub down the injury with ice and ice packs. For both treatments ice cubes, such as the ones made in the refrigerator, are needed. In an ice pack, the cubes are smashed into smaller pieces, packed into a bag or a handerkerchief and laid on the injured area. The pack should remain there for about 2-3 hours. It is important that the treatment is administered straight after the injury and not several hours later. The formation of a bruise can also be checked by using a tight pressure bandage. Creams that inflame the skin and the consumption of alcohol are to be avoided in all circumstances, since they enlarge blood vessels and increase internal bleeding.

When rubbing down with ice, the injured area should be treated with whole ice cubes, also over a period of several hours. If the injured area is cooled down to almost 0°C, this brings about an astonishingly rapid recovery, as mentioned before.

Heat packs
After 24 to 48 hours, when the injured area is at normal body temperature again, bruises and pulled ligaments or muscles can be given heat treatment. Special deep action is obtained by using heat packs. A dark glutinous paste is heated up to about 50°-60°C, packed in plastic film and laid on the injured areas as hot as is bearable. The pack itself is covered by cloths to keep in the heat. The treatment lasts

Sporting injuries

approximately 20-30 minutes and can with a little practice be carried out by the injured player.

Massage
The healing process can be helped by stroking, kneading, pummeling, rubbing and shaking. As a rule, this classic massaging is only done by qualified masseurs at the right time and in the right manner. Experienced sportsmen can, however, employ the techniques themselves and thereby speed up the healing process. The lymph vessel massage should be left to a qualified masseur. Pumping movements in a certain rhythm cause lymph fluid to flow from the injured area painlessly and soothingly at an early stage. The same is inevitably true for underwater massage. Treatment is given at a predetermined pressure according to the width of the water jet used.

Other methods of treatment
A number of further possible treatments are reserved for the physiotherapist. In suction-wave massage a vacuum is created under a bell jar and the tissue is then 'aired'. The resulting increase in circulation and in material replacement quickens the healing of pulled capsules, sprains, bruises, torn muscles, etc.

Treatment using stimulating currents and ultra-sound is among the most modern of methods. This has surprisingly rapid and successful results.

Therapeutic exercises
The patient himself can make a definite contribution to the treatments described above. As soon as he can move the injured part of the body again, he should start therapeutic exercises immediately. Swimming, cycling, running and gymnastic exercises up to the moment of pain quicken the removal of damaged pieces of tissue, increase circulation and thereby the introduction of healthy replacement material, and do not hinder the muscles hardening and building up again. These therapeutic exercises can contribute decisively to the rapid healing of the patient's injury. Of course this individual therapy should be talked over with a doctor or masseur.

Pulling a muscle
If a player does not warm up sufficiently, or he has a muscle injury that has not healed properly, or if single groups of muscles have seized because of overloading or salt loss from heavy sweating, he will first feel a slight pulling in the muscle. This symptom grows more intense with a sudden burst of speed, a

Methods of treatment

change of direction, a shooting or a lunging movement to become a stabbing pain. Individual bundles of muscle are stretched beyond the limit of their elasticity without haemorrhaging; if there is further loading, there is a great danger that the muscle will tear.

Initial treatment
As soon as the first pulling pain is felt, stop playing and try to release tension in the muscles by stroking and massaging to relax them. As a precaution put on a support bandage or a tape bandage. If the pain increases, stop playing altogether.

Further treatment
Firstly rub down with ice; after approximately 2-3 hours apply a damp heat compress and after 24 hours manual massage and electrotherapy. Try therapeutic exercises early on up to the moment of pain, first putting on support bandages.

Tearing a muscle
If strains increase above those causing the pulled muscle, individual muscle bundles can tear. Shooting pains that often make it impossible to move the injured part point to muscle-tearing. The injured area is often soft and spongy. After some hours an indentation under the skin can frequently be seen and felt. Heavy bruising is always connected with muscle tears.

Initial treatment
Cool with ice for up to one hour and put on a compression bandage.

Further treatment
Only after 24 hours, then ice-massaging every day if possible or cold swirling baths (10 minutes); light massage of lymph vessels, ultra-sound or stimulating current treatment. From the third and fourth day isometric tensing exercises; and light training only from the eighth day.

Joint sprains
The parts of the bones that form the joints can be twisted round, pushed or opened out by powerful exterior influences. But they quickly snap back again into their original position. According to the severity and situation of the injury, the capsule ligament structure, tendons and muscles, blood and lymph vessels can be injured as well as the cartilage and bone parts. The severe pain is generally accompanied by heavy swelling and bruise formation. These both lead to the joint being temporarily incapable of functioning.

Initial treatment
Avoid any further strain on the

Sporting injuries

joint, rest up the injured part of the body and immediately restrict the formation of a bruise with a cooling compression bandage.

Further treatment
Find a doctor for an X-ray, then rest to prevent inner secondary haemorrhaging; and back up the treatment with ice massages. Allow the masseur to massage away damaged pieces of tissue bordering on the muscles. Stimulating current, ultra-sound and suction-wave treatment later on. Therapeutic exercises only when the injured part of the body is pain-free when resting. Increase the extent and intensity of movement slowly.

Pulling ligaments
The tendons connecting the two bony parts of a joint (for example, the inside and outside ligaments on the knee joint and the side ligaments on the ankle joint) can be overstretched, like the muscles, and pulled. Pulling a ligament is bound up with severe pains at the base of the ligament, limitation of use and, contrary to when a muscle is pulled, heavy swelling.

Initial treatment
Cooling with an ice bag.

Further treatment
If the ligaments are badly torn, the joint must be kept still for at least 14 days with a plaster-cast; support bandages are not sufficient for this. If ligaments are not too badly torn, they can be treated with most heat, hot air with a moist compress or contrast (heat/ice) therapy; later electro, suction-wave and ultra-sound treatment as well. Massage only in the adjoining muscle region.

Therapeutic exercises to a reasonable extent, but initially only isometric exercises to strengthen the muscles supporting the ligament structure.

Meniscus injuries
The meniscus consists of one horn-shaped and one half-moon-shaped disc of cartilage. The two discs have the job of balancing out the inequalities of the joint-forming bony parts of the knee joint. Meniscus injuries come about mostly when the knee joint is bent or stretched and twisted round at the same time, with the sole of the foot rigid. Meniscus injuries must always be treated by a doctor and in severe cases can only be remedied by an operation.

Distinguishing features
Players and trainers must become familiar with the following symptoms of meniscus injury:
- joint is locked, ie it is

Methods of treatment

impossible to bend or stretch out the leg
- the player cannot stand or walk on his injured leg
- sudden stabbing pains when kicking the ball, particularly with the inside of the instep
- stabbing pain when the body is twisted sideways

Injury to the Achilles tendon
The Achilles tendon can be severely injured or chronically overloaded, causing considerable pain. In this way the tendon sheath or the tendon itself can be irritated and inflamed. If it is chronically over-strained, in the end the tendon can be torn – even torn away completely.

Causes of tearing the Achilles tendon are frequent distortions of the foot, for example one leg too short or a hollow foot, wrong footwear or chronic overloading.

Initial treatment
The muscles adjoining the Achilles tendon must be eased by raising your shoes or boots.

Further treatment
Rubbing down with ice, also alternate heat and ice treatment as shock therapy.

After the ice treatment, stretching the Achilles tendon and manual massage of the fibula muscles by a masseur. In addition, ultra-sound and suction-wave treatment.

First-aid equipment

To be able to carry out the types of initial care and further treatment mentioned above, a well-equipped first-aid kit is necessary. There is a difference between the minimum equipment that players and trainers always have with them and the special equipment that trained masseurs have in large cases.

The player's equipment
1 bandage, 6cm wide
1 adhesive bandage, 8cm wide
1 roll of Elastoplast, 5m x 2½cm
1 small bottle of massage oil, in summer 1 bottle of cooling liniment
Footspray for prevention of fungal infections rampant in all changing or locker rooms
Possibly knee or ankle bandage stockings in case of chronic joint damage or after severe injury.

Additional trainer's equipment
Gauze bandages, Elastoplast in various widths, cotton wool (absorbent cotton) for checking the flow of blood, additional elastic adhesive bandages, surgical spirit, various ointments and pain-killing pills.

Sporting injuries

Masseur's equipment
The trained masseur also takes a large number of other supplies with him when he accompanies a team to a match or particularly when on tour. The first-aid case pictured below shows a small selection of the sports masseur's extensive assortment. In addition there is fixed apparatus for the different types of physiotherapy.

A first-aid case packed with everything necessary for the initial treatment of injuries as instructed above.

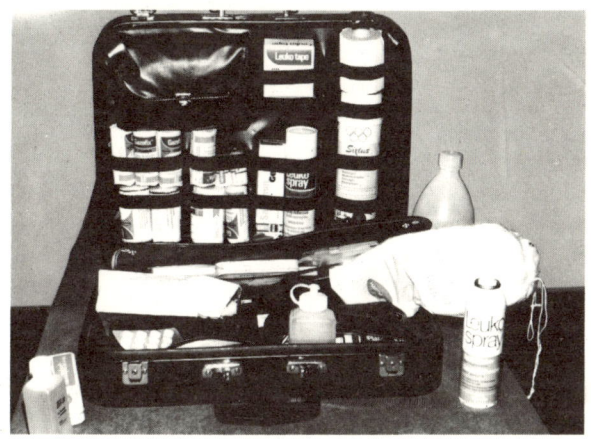

Rules of the game

The history of the game can also be studied as the development of its rules. Today's include 17 single rules and a whole number of individual regulations.

Whereas the rules that are valid today have been in existence for centuries, apart from some individual exceptions, the rules in the early history developed erratically. Much of what every buff knows today has arisen during the course of this century; just as many regulations were altered or have completely disappeared.

The first rules of modern times were drawn up in 1846 by Cambridge University students. According to these, 15-20 players could make up a team; the number of players was not restricted to 11 until 1870. When the Football Association was founded in 1863 and was separated from rugby football, handball was still allowed. In 1868 it was decided that players had to wear trousers that reached below the knee and cover their heads with tasselled caps.

Finally in 1870 handball was banned for all players and in 1871 the goalkeeper was allowed to use his hands in defence. The crossbar was introduced in 1875; previously only a belt of material had been used. The referee was granted sole authority over decision making in 1889, where previously he was only allowed to punish violations of the rules by complaining to the team captains. In 1891 the penalty kick was generally introduced.

In 1903 handball by the goalkeeper was limited to the penalty area: previously he could use his hands for defence in the whole of his team's half of the pitch. The regulation about knee-length trousers was lifted again by 1904. In 1913, through the introduction of the 10-yard (9.15 metre) rule, it was laid down that a 'suitable distance' was to be kept between the ball placed ready for a free kick and the opposition. In 1921 a dark yellow pullover was prescribed for goalkeepers to distinguish them from the rest of the team. In 1925 the offside rule that is basically the one laid down today in Rule 11 took over the Nottingham offside rule, which had been valid until then.

Rules of the game

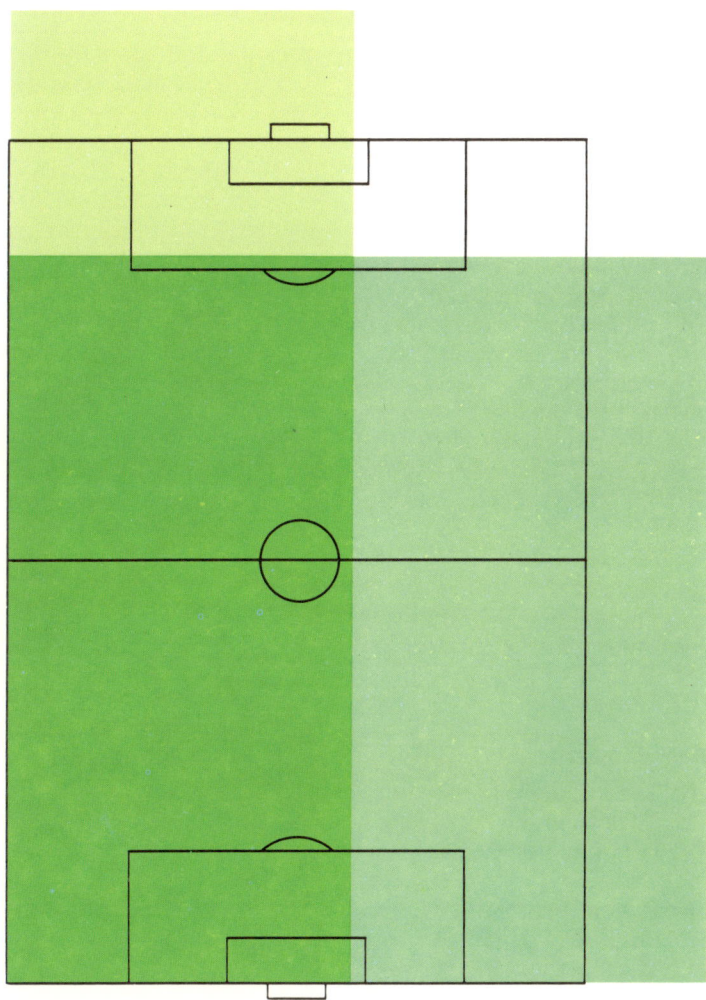

The size of the pitch and the ratio between length and width are not laid down precisely. The length can fluctuate between 90 and 120m and the width between 45 and 90m. Concerning the ratio of length to width, the rules only state that the pitch must be longer than it is broad. It is thanks to this idiosyncratic, flexible rule that official pitches can be laid out where the available playing surface clearly varies from the normal 69 x 105m measurements.

Rules of the game

In 1951 football adapted itself to the age of television. Now the ball has to be white or multi-coloured. In 1966 it was allowed — first in England and later on the whole FIFA area – that two players could be substituted during the game, even if they were not injured. Later on the goalkeeper's freedom of movement was limited to four paces to prevent so-called 'playing for time'.

The development of the rules has certainly not finished even today, but a fundamental change in the 17 rules below is unlikely in the foreseeable future.

The 17 rules are:
1 The pitch
2 The ball
3 The number of players
4 The player's equipment
5 The referee
6 The linesmen
7 The length of the game
8 The beginning of the game
9 The ball in and out of play
10 How a goal is scored
11 Offside
12 Banned play and unsportsmanlike acts
13 The free kick
14 The penalty kick
15 The throw-in
16 The goal kick
17 The corner kick

Rules of the game

Rule 1

Information has already been given on the dimensions of the pitch, ie the length of the sides and goal lines, in the drawing on page 99 and the text that goes with it. In each half of the pitch goal areas, penalty areas and corners have been drawn in as well. A centre circle with a radius of 9.15 metres is drawn round the central spot on the pitch. All pitch boundaries are marked by lines 12cm wide and the four corners of the pitch by a flag at least 1.5 metres in height in addition. The goals consist of two vertical posts and a horizontal crossbar which can be square-edged or round and must be 10-12cm in diameter.

Rule 2

The ball must be spherical and have a circumference of 68-71cm and a weight of 396-453g. Junior balls have a circumference of 62-66cm and weigh 340-390g.

Rule 3

The number of players who actively take part in the game must not exceed 11 per team; one of them is the goalkeeper. According to the rules, two players can be substituted at any time in the game. In friendly games up to five players can be substituted. A swop between goalkeeper and outfield player is possible during break in play if the linesman is informed.

Rule 4

The players' equipment must not include anything that could endanger another player. Footwear is not compulsory. Studs can be made of leather, rubber, plastic or aluminium; their diameter should not be less than 12.7mm and they should not be more than 19mm long. The goalkeeper's clothes should stand out from those of the outfield players. Black is reserved for the officials, and not even the goalkeeper is allowed to wear a black pullover.

Rule 5

The referee has to enforce the rules of the game and decide any disputed points. In particular he has to refrain from imposing penalties in all cases where he is convinced that he would be creating an advantage for the team that has broken the rules of the game. He has to make notes on the course of the game, control playing time and allow any lost time to be played afterwards.

He has the power to interrupt the game or call it off completely at any time because of a violation

Rules of the game

of the rules, bad weather, disturbances from spectators or for other reasons. From the moment he steps on the pitch he has the right to caution a player for improper or unsportsmanlike actions and to bar him from further participation in the game if a repetition occurs. He is allowed to prevent any other people, apart from the players and linesmen, from coming on to the pitch.

He has to stop play if in his opinion a player is seriously injured. He has to send off any player who in his opinion is guilty of an act of violence, serious foul play or insulting remarks. After each interruption he gives the signal for play to continue. He decides whether the ball conforms to the rules and can be used for play.

Black is reserved for the vests and shirts of the referee and the two linesmen.

Rule 6

The linesmen have to show when the ball goes out of play and which team is entitled to a corner kick, goal kick or throw-in. They help the referee to run the game in accordance with the rules. The referee can relieve a linesmen who in his opinion is not capable of carrying out his duties and decide on a replacement.

Rule 7

The length of the game: the game consists, when no other arrangement has been made, of two halves each of 45 minutes duration. Lost playing time must be made up in the appropriate half. Playing time for junior teams is normally shortened by 5 minutes per playing half. Normally half-time should not exceed 10 minutes, unless it is with the referee's agreement. In cup matches, different regulations apply according to the competition. In home tournaments of a single leg, if the tie is drawn it is first replayed on the ground of the team that was originally drawn away; subsequent replays are normally played on neutral territory until one team is the winner. The result of two-leg ties is based on the aggregate score after the two matches. In some cases extra time is played – of two 15-minute periods – after a short break. In European competitions, penalty kicks may be taken to decide the result if the scores are level at the end of extra time.

Rule 8

The beginning of the game is announced by the referee's signal. Before the beginning of the game, a coin is tossed to

Rules of the game

decide which half each team will start off in or who kicks off. Whoever wins the toss can choose between the half of the pitch or the kick-off. To start the game there is a kick-off in which one player kicks the ball from the centre spot into the opponents' half of the field. At the kick-off the ball is only in play when it has covered the same distance as its circumference. A goal cannot be scored direct from a kick-off.

After a goal has been scored, the game is restarted in the same way by one player from the team against which the goal was scored. After half-time a player from the team that did not kick off at the beginning of the game restarts play.

Rule 9

1 The ball is out of the game when all of it has crossed over the goal or touchline either on the ground or in the air or when the referee has stopped play.
2 The ball is in the game at all other times, even when it rebounds off the goal posts, the crossbar, the corner flag or an official (on the field of play) on to the pitch.

Rule 10

A goal is scored when a ball played according to the rules has crossed over the goal line between the goal posts and under the crossbar completely, ie its full diameter. The team that has scored the most goals in one game – or tie – is the winner. When no goal has been scored or when both teams have scored the same number of goals, the game is regarded as being 'drawn'.

Rule 11

A player is offside when he is nearer the opponents' goal line than the ball at the moment the ball is being being played.
There are four exceptions:
- the player is in his own half of the field
- two players from the opposing team are nearer their goal line than the striker
- the ball has been touched or played last by an opponent
- the ball comes straight from a corner kick, goal kick, throw-in or a drop-ball (referee's ball).

Rules of the game

Violations against these rules are punished with a free kick. A player in an offside position as such should not be penalised when he is not in the referee's opinion interfering with play or an opponent, ie when he can gain no advantage from his offside position. The outline on this page shows the two basic positions that are determined by the offside rule. In the following diagrams and the corresponding parts of the text, special situations are deal with in which the offside ruling is disputed again and again.

At the moment the ball is passed, player A2 is in the offside position, likewise player A3 who is at the same level with the last but one defender; striker A4, however, is not offside.

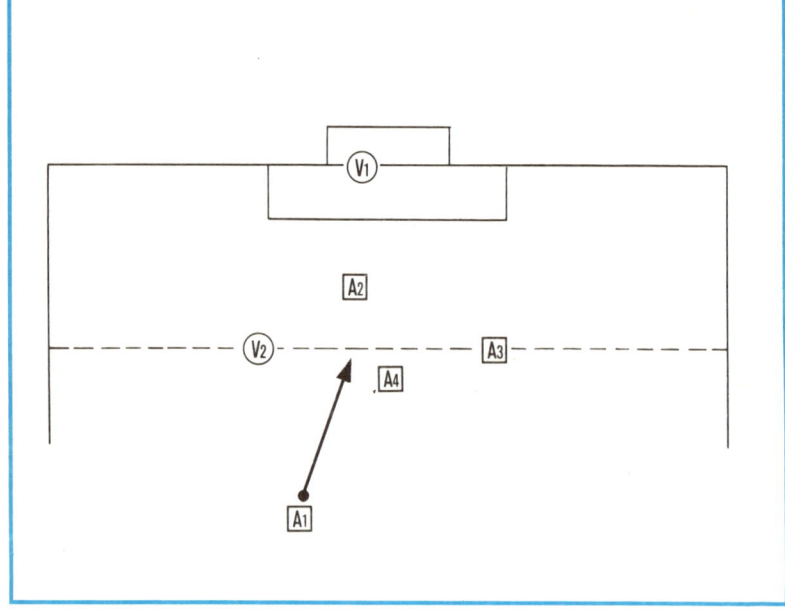

Rules of the game

A2 is not offside
At the moment when A1 passed the ball he was not closer to the opponents' goal line than the ball. If A2 had been in the A2' position when the ball was passed, he would have been offside.

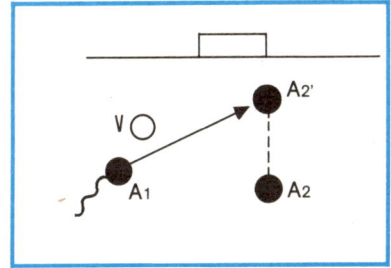

A2 is not offside
Since A1 is waiting to pass until A2 has run back to the A2' position, A2's original 'offside' is not penalised.

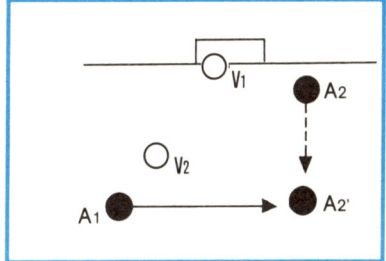

A2 is not offside
A1 shoots at goal, but A2 is not offside at this point. After A1's shot, A2 runs into an offside position (A2') and the shot bounces away from V1. Not offside, since the ball was last played by the opponent and A2 was not in an offside position when the shot was made.

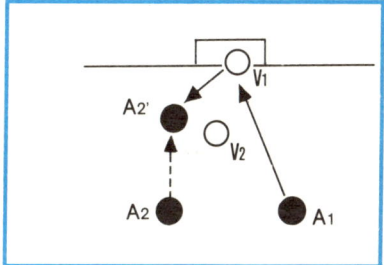

A2 is not offside
'Offside' is not punished from a corner kick. The next ball contact is made by opponent V2, ie the ball comes from the opponent, so that here also A2's 'offside' does not result in a penalty.

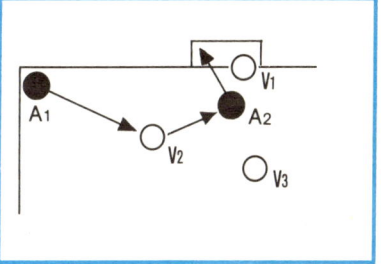

Rules of the game

Rule 12

This establishes what constitutes banned play and unsportsmanlike actions; it is therefore in practice the most important rule. Accordingly, a player is punished by a direct free kick to the opposing side when he purposely:
- kicks or tries to kick an opponent
- deliberately trips an opponent
- jumps at an opponent
- jostles an opponent
- jostles an opponent in a vigorous or dangerous manner
- pushes an opponent from behind when the latter is not blocking him
- strikes or tries to strike an opponent
- holds on to an opponent
- pushes an opponent
- deliberately touches the ball with his hands (exception being the goalkeeper in his own penalty area).

If a player commits one of the above offences on purpose in his own penalty area, he is punished by a penalty kick; this is regardless of where the ball is at the time.

A player is punished by an indirect free kick when he:
- plays in a dangerous manner
- jostles incorrectly without the ball being within reach
- blocks his opponent without trying to go for the ball
- jostles the goalkeeper except when the latter is holding the ball, or hinders an opponent or has left his own goal area
- the goalkeeper takes more than four paces with the ball without releasing it
- the goalkeeper in the referee's opinion slows down the game

Comment

Rule 12 names nine offences that are considered as 'unfair play'. In any case the prerequisite for these is that they are committed on purpose, ie negligently or with lack of foresight. An example may clarify this. Point 9 of Rule 12 forbids the ball to be held on to, thrown, carried or hit with the hand or arm – please note, on purpose. Now the example. A player falls in his own goal area and instinctively puts out his hand to the ground to check his fall. At that moment the ball strikes his hand. Although a certain goal is saved by the handball, the referee should not blow for a penalty because the player did not touch the ball with his hand on purpose. The referee must make this decision in a split second. This is certainly a difficult job, since he must come to a decision without the help of 'slow motion' film.

Rules of the game

Causing a fall
Although the player rushing in is trying to reach the ball, a direct free kick is awarded as the opponent's supporting leg is caught, making him fall.

Jumping and pushing
The forward jumps against the goalkeeper and hits him with an outstretched arm. Both offences are punished with a direct free kick.

From dangerous to banned play
An outstretched leg as such is not considered dangerous play. But since it is certainly coming into contact with the body, this method is banned and punished with a direct free kick.

Advantage
The player rushing in has tried to bring down his opponent, but he arrives too late as the opponent and the ball are already past. The referee uses the advantage rule here and allows play to continue, although an offence has been committed.

Rules of the game

Rule 13

There are two types of free kick that the referee can award:
- direct free kick; a goal can be scored direct from it without another player having to touch the ball
- indirect free kick: a goal can only be scored from it when the ball is touched by another player first.

When taking a free kick, no player in the opposing team is allowed nearer than 9.15 metres – he can, however, stand on his own goal line when an indirect free kick is taken in the penalty area. When a free kick is taken, the ball must be stationary; it is only in play when it has covered the same distance as its circumference. The player taking the free kick is only allowed to touch the ball again after another player has touched it. Offences against these regulations are punished with an indirect free kick.

If players come nearer than 9.15 metres to the ball before the free kick has been taken, the referee should delay the free kick until the offending player retreats the required distance. If he does not, he can be cautioned.

Rule 14

Direct free kicks are taken as penalties when the offence takes place in the penalty area. When it is being taken, all players with the exception of the player taking the penalty and the opposing goalkeeper must be on the pitch but outside the penalty area and at least 9.15 metres from the penalty spot – until the ball has rolled its circumference.

The goalkeeper must stand stationary on his goal line between the posts until the ball is kicked. The ball must be kicked forward. The offside rule is not involved with a penalty kick; all players apart from the goalkeeper must be behind the ball.

Rule 15

A throw-in is given when the ball has crossed over the touchline completely, either along the ground or in the air. The throw-in is given to the team that did not touch the ball last. The player taking the throw-in must turn his face towards the pitch at the moment of the throw-in and stand with a part of each foot on or outside the touchline.

The throw-in must be made with both hands above the head. The player throwing in must not play the ball before another player has touched it. A goal cannot be scored direct from a throw-in. If the throw-in is illegal, the opposing team is awarded a

Rules of the game

throw-in.
Important: At the moment the throw-in is being taken, the offside rule does not apply. This can therefore be used for sudden attacks.

Rule 16

A goal kick is given when the ball goes completely over the goal line either in the air or along the ground and when it has been touched last by a player of the attacking team. With a goal kick the ball is in play when it leaves the penalty area. If it does not do this, the goal kick must be taken again. A goal cannot be scored direct from a goal kick. When a goal kick is being taken, the opposing players must be outside the penalty area. The player who is taking the goal kick is only allowed to play the ball again when another player has touched it.

The goal kick is taken from the ground in the goal area; the goalkeeper is not allowed to punt the ball upfield.

Rule 17

A corner is granted when the ball goes completely over the goal line either in the air or along the ground and has been touched last by a player in the defending team. The corner kick is taken, with the ball stationary, from inside the quarter-circle and on the side of the goal where the ball went out.

When the corner kick is being taken, the corner flag should not be removed and opposing players must remain at least 9.15 metres away from the ball until the corner kick has been taken. The player taking the corner kick is only allowed to play the ball again when another player has touched it. A goal can be scored direct from a corner kick.

The winners

World Cup

1930 in Uruguay – Uruguay
1934 in Italy – Italy
1938 in France – Italy
1950 in Brazil – Uruguay
1954 in Switzerland – West Germany
1958 in Sweden – Brazil
1962 in Chile – Brazil
1966 in England – England
1970 in Mexico – Brazil
1974 in West Germany – West Germany
1978 in Argentina – Argentina

European Nations Cup

1960 USSR
1964 Spain
1968 Italy
1972 West Germany
1976 Czechoslovakia
1980 West Germany

European Cup

1956 Real Madrid
1957 Real Madrid
1958 Real Madrid
1959 Real Madrid
1960 Real Madrid
1961 Benfica
1962 Benfica
1963 AC Milan
1964 Internazionale
1965 Internazionale
1966 Real Madrid
1967 Celtic
1968 Manchester United
1969 AC Milan
1970 Feyenoord
1971 Ajax Amsterdam
1972 Ajax Amsterdam
1973 Ajax Amsterdam
1974 Bayern Munich
1975 Bayern Munich
1976 Bayern Munich
1977 Liverpool
1978 Liverpool
1979 Nottingham Forest
1980 Nottingham Forest
1981 Liverpool

European Cup Winners Cup

1961 Fiorentina
1962 Atletico Madrid
1963 Tottenham Hotspur
1964 Sporting Portugal
1965 West Ham United
1966 Borussia Dortmund
1967 Bayern Munich
1968 AC Milan
1969 Slovan Bratislava
1970 Manchester City
1971 Chelsea
1972 Glasgow Rangers
1973 AC Milan
1974 FC Magdeburg
1975 Dynamo Kiev
1976 Anderlecht
1977 SV Hamburg
1978 Anderlecht
1979 Barcelona
1980 Valencia
1981 Dynamo Tiblisi

Inter Cities Fairs Cup

1958 Barcelona
1960 Barcelona
1961 AS Roma
1962 Valencia
1963 Valencia
1964 Real Zaragoza

The winners

1965 Ferencvaros
1966 Barcelona
1967 Dynamo Zagreb
1968 Leeds United
1969 Newcastle United
1970 Arsenal
1971 Leeds United

UEFA Cup

1972 Tottenham Hotspur
1973 Liverpool
1974 Feyenoord
1975 Borussia Monchengladbach
1976 Liverpool
1977 Juventus
1978 PSV Eindhoven
1979 Borussia Monchengladbach
1980 Eintracht Frankfurt
1981 Ipswich

Home International Championship

1884 Scotland
1885 Scotland
1886 England/Scotland
1887 Scotland
1888 England
1889 Scotland
1890 England/Scotland
1891 England
1892 England
1893 England
1894 Scotland
1895 England
1896 Scotland
1897 Scotland
1898 England
1899 England
1900 Scotland
1901 England
1902 Scotland
1903 England/Ireland/Scotland
1904 England
1905 England
1906 England/Scotland
1907 Wales
1908 England/Scotland
1909 England
1910 Scotland
1911 England
1912 England/Scotland
1913 England
1914 Ireland
1915-19 not played
1920 Wales
1921 Scotland
1922 Scotland
1923 Scotland
1924 Wales
1925 Scotland
1926 Scotland
1927 England/Scotland
1928 Wales
1929 Scotland
1930 England
1931 England/Scotland
1932 England
1933 Wales
1934 Wales
1935 England/Scotland
1936 Scotland
1937 Wales
1938 England
1939 England/Scotland/Wales
1940-46 not played
1947 England
1948 England
1949 Scotland
1950 England
1951 Scotland
1952 England/Wales
1953 England/Scotland
1954 England
1955 England

The winners

1956 England/Ireland/Scotland/Wales
1957 England
1958 England/Ireland
1959 England/Ireland
1960 England/Scotland/Wales
1961 England
1962 Scotland
1963 Scotland
1964 England/Ireland/Scotland
1965 England
1966 England
1967 Scotland
1968 England
1969 England
1970 England/Scotland/Wales
1971 England
1972 England/Scotland
1973 England
1974 England/Scotland
1975 England
1976 Scotland
1977 Scotland
1978 England
1979 England
1980 Northern Ireland
1981 Void

English Football League

1889 Preston North End
1890 Preston North End
1891 Everton
1892 Sunderland
1893 Sunderland
1894 Aston Villa
1895 Sunderland
1896 Aston Villa
1897 Aston Villa
1898 Sheffield United
1899 Aston Villa
1900 Aston Villa
1901 Liverpool
1902 Sunderland
1903 The Wednesday
1904 The Wednesday
1905 Newcastle United
1906 Liverpool
1907 Newcastle United
1908 Manchester United
1909 Newcastle United
1910 Aston Villa
1911 Manchester United
1912 Blackburn Rovers
1913 Sunderland
1914 Blackburn Rovers
1915 Everton
1916-19 not played
1920 West Bromwich Albion
1921 Burnley
1922 Liverpool
1923 Liverpool
1924 Huddersfield Town
1925 Huddersfield Town
1926 Huddersfield Town
1927 Newcastle United
1928 Everton
1929 Sheffield Wednesday
1930 Sheffield Wednesday
1931 Arsenal
1932 Everton
1933 Arsenal
1934 Arsenal
1935 Arsenal
1936 Sunderland
1937 Manchester City
1938 Arsenal
1939 Everton
1940-46 not played
1947 Liverpool
1948 Arsenal
1949 Portsmouth
1950 Portsmouth
1951 Tottenham Hotspur
1952 Manchester United
1953 Arsenal
1954 Wolverhampton Wanderers
1955 Chelsea

The winners

1956	Manchester United
1957	Manchester United
1958	Wolverhampton Wanderers
1959	Wolverhampton Wanderers
1960	Burnley
1961	Tottenham Hotspur
1962	Ipswich Town
1963	Everton
1964	Liverpool
1965	Manchester United
1966	Liverpool
1967	Manchester United
1968	Manchester City
1969	Leeds United
1970	Everton
1971	Arsenal
1972	Derby County
1973	Liverpool
1974	Leeds United
1975	Derby County
1976	Liverpool
1977	Liverpool
1978	Nottingham Forest
1979	Liverpool
1980	Liverpool
1981	Aston Villa

FA Cup

1872	Wanderers
1873	Wanderers
1874	Oxford University
1875	Royal Engineers
1876	Wanderers
1877	Wanderers
1878	Wanderers
1879	Old Etonians
1880	Clapham Rovers
1881	Old Carthusians
1882	Old Etonians
1883	Blackburn Olympic
1884	Blackburn Rovers
1885	Blackburn Rovers
1886	Blackburn Rovers
1887	Aston Villa
1888	West Bromwich Albion
1889	Preston North End
1890	Blackburn Rovers
1891	Blackburn Rovers
1892	West Bromwich Albion
1893	Wolverhampton Wanderers
1894	Notts County
1895	Aston Villa
1896	The Wednesday
1897	Aston Villa
1898	Nottingham Forest
1899	Sheffield United
1900	Bury
1901	Tottenham Hotspur
1902	Sheffield United
1903	Bury
1904	Manchester City
1905	Aston Villa
1906	Everton
1907	The Wednesday
1908	Wolverhampton Wanderers
1909	Manchester United
1910	Newcastle United
1911	Bradford City
1912	Barnsley
1913	Aston Villa
1914	Burnley
1915	Sheffield United
1916-19	not played
1920	Aston Villa
1921	Tottenham Hotspur
1922	Huddersfield Town
1923	Bolton Wanderers
1924	Newcastle United
1925	Sheffield United
1926	Bolton Wanderers
1927	Cardiff City
1928	Blackburn Rovers
1929	Bolton Wanderers
1930	Arsenal
1931	West Bromwich Albion
1932	Newcastle United

The winners

1933 Everton
1934 Manchester City
1935 Sheffield Wednesday
1936 Arsenal
1937 Sunderland
1938 Preston North End
1939 Portsmouth
1940-45 not played
1946 Derby County
1947 Charlton Athletic
1948 Manchester United
1949 Wolverhampton Wanderers
1950 Arsenal
1951 Newcastle United
1952 Newcastle United
1953 Blackpool
1954 West Bromwich Albion
1955 Newcastle United
1956 Manchester City
1957 Aston Villa
1958 Bolton Wanderers
1959 Nottingham Forest
1960 Wolverhampton Wanderers
1961 Tottenham Hotspur
1962 Tottenham Hotspur
1963 Manchester United
1964 West Ham United
1965 Liverpool
1966 Everton
1967 Tottenham Hotspur
1968 West Bromwich Albion
1969 Manchester City
1970 Chelsea
1971 Arsenal
1972 Leeds United
1973 Sunderland
1974 Liverpool
1975 West Ham United
1976 Southampton
1977 Manchester United
1978 Ipswich
1979 Arsenal
1980 West Ham United
1981 Tottenham Hotspur

Famous names in the game

Banks, Gordon

England
One of the stars of England's World Cup winning side in 1966, confirming his status as one of the world's leading goalkeepers in the 1970 World Cup. Began his career with Chesterfield (1958) and went to Leicester the following season. In 1963 he won his first cap for England against Brazil. In 1967 he was transferred to Stoke City. Elected English Footballer of the Year in 1972. Recovered from an eye injury following a car crash and then played in the United States.

Beckenbauer, Franz

West Germany
Sweeper for Bayern Munich for 13 years. In May 1977 he was sensationally transferred to New York Cosmos. German international with a record 109 caps, he played in all major competitions with Bayern and West Germany.

World Cup championship 1974; European Nations Cup 1972; European Cup 1967, 1974, 1975 and 1976; European Footballer of the Year 1972; West German League championship 1969, 1972, 1973 and 1974; German Federal League Cup 1966, 1967, 1969 and 1971; German Footballer of the Year 1966, 1968, 1972 and 1976.

In 1977 he won a North American championship medal with New York Cosmos.

Beckenbauer has won more medals than any other German player, including Seeler, Walter, Rahn and others. Overwhelmed with awards of all types from the association, league, state and the sporting press, the nickname 'Kaiser' given him by the national sporting press is the most characteristic. As captain of the national side, he enjoyed a previously unknown command over the other players and also earned his nickname because of his inimitable, elegant style of play.

Best, George

Northern Ireland
His magical skills made him a soccer idol in the 1960s and early 1970s, highlighted when he helped his club Manchester United to a European Cup triumph against Benfica in 1968, when he scored a brilliant solo goal in the 4-1 win. That year he was voted European and English Footballer of the Year. He won two championship medals with United – in 1965 and 1967 – and has been capped for Northern Ireland 35 times.

The pressures of stardom sadly

117

Famous names in the game

led to his premature retirement in 1972, although he later made a come-back with Los Angeles Aztecs (whom he joined in 1976), Fulham and Hibernian.

A member of the San Jose Earthquakes since 1980, 'Bestie' is the team captain and assistant coach as well as the club's leader in the middle of the field. He has been among the North American Soccer League's top point-producers and was voted his team's most valuable player by local fans and team-mates alike.

Blanchflower, Danny

Northern Ireland
Skilful right half, who started his career with Glentoran before moving to Barnsley and then Aston Villa (1951-54), finally settling with Tottenham Hotspur. He won 56 caps for Northern Ireland and was voted English Footballer of the Year in 1958 and again in 1961 – the year Spurs won the double of league championship and FA Cup. Under his captaincy they went on to win the cup again the following year and the European Cup Winners Cup in 1963. He has since briefly managed – the Northern Ireland side and Chelsea.

Cajkovski, Zlatko

Yugoslavia
Great captain of the Yugoslavian national side from 1946 to 1955, with 57 caps. After his playing career was over 'Tschik' (cigarette end) – as he was jokingly called – became just as successful as a coach, leading 1st Cologne and Bayern Munich to victories in the German league championships. Under him, Bayern Munich also won the European Cup Winners Cup. He then coached in Greece, where he again achieved championship success.

Charlton, Bobby

England
Manchester United and England player (106 caps), arguably the most popular player of modern times – together with Sir Stanley Matthews. Played for his only club between 1955 and 1973. World Cup championship 1966; European Cup 1968; league championship 1957, 1965 and 1967; FA Cup 1963. European and English Footballer of the Year in 1966.

Scored 49 goals for England, many of them with his spectacular left-foot shooting. His defence-splitting passes, clever flicks and remarkable feinting, dribbling and acceleration made him one of

Famous names in the game

the most respected English players of the late 1950s and 1960s. Survivor of the Munich air disaster in 1958, he was crucial in Matt Busby's revival plans. Briefly player-manager of Preston North End after leaving United.

Coluna, Mario

Portugal
Won a record 73 caps between 1954 and 1966. Began as a centre forward, but it was as a midfield player that he helped Benfica to three consecutive European Cup finals in the early 1960s and again in 1968. Under his leadership, Portugal got as far as the quarter-finals in the 1966 World Cup.

Cramer, Dettmar

West Germany
Coach for FIFA from 1967 to 1974, he was one of the best-known German coaches in the world of top-class soccer. Top coach in the West German Football League from 1949 to 1963, he worked in many countries all over the world before moving to Bayern Munich in 1975. He took over the team when it was in a critical state and led it to victory in the European Cup in 1975 and 1976. But even Cramer, who was given the nickname of the 'runner meter' because of his small figure, suffered the cruel blows of fate when he was relieved of his job with Bayern after they were relegated. His example proves that even the so-called 'top' coaches and managers do not always have the same success with each team – and particularly not over a period of seasons.

Cruyff, Johan

Holland
Holland's most celebrated player, whose ability is only surpassed by his financial genius. From 1963 to 1973 he was the star of Ajax Amsterdam, then went to Barcelona until 1976. From 1967 to 1976 he won 46 caps for Holland, who were runners-up in the World Cup in 1974 and third in the European Nations Cup in 1976.

European Cup with Ajax in 1971, 1972 and 1973; Dutch league championship in 1966, 1967, 1968, 1970, 1972 and 1973; Spanish league championship with Barcelona in 1974. European Footballer of the Year in 1971.

Famous names in the game

Didi
(Waldyr Pereira)

Brazil

Captain of the Brazilian side that won the World Cup in 1958 and 1962. He was capped 55 times between 1952 and 1962 and played for Madureiro, Botafoga and Real Madrid. In 1970 he proved his tactical skills as coach of the Peruvian national side in the World Cup in Mexico, leading the rank outsiders to the quarter-finals.

Eusebio
(Eusebio Silva Ferreira)

Portugal

One of the great players of all time and regarded by many as successor to Pele. Goal king of the 1966 World Cup in England. A dynamic player with a very powerful shot, he dominated the game between 1965 and 1973. He led Benfica to victory against Real Madrid in the European Cup in 1962. After an illustrious career in Spanish soccer, he went to play in the United States

Greaves, Jimmy

England

Played league soccer from 1957 to 1971, scoring 491 goals – 357 for Chelsea, Tottenham Hotspur and West Ham, 47 for England (for whom he won 57 caps) and 9 while playing briefly for AC Milan. In his day he was one of the sharpest men in front of goal and was the league's top scorer five times. With Tottenham he won two FA Cup medals (1962 and 1967) and a European Cup Winners Cup medal in 1963.

Greenwood, Ron

England

Manager of the England national side since 1977, having previously managed West Ham for more than 16 years. Played as centre half for Chelsea, Bradford, Brentford and Fulham. With West Ham, his style of soccer – flowing and attacking – was well-known. Under his guidance England qualified for the World cup in 1982, the first time in 12 years they have appeared in the final stages of the competition.

Hamrin, Kurre

Sweden

Apart form a spell with AIK Stockholm, Hamrin played most of his soccer in Italy with Juventus, Padova, Fiorentina, AC Milan and Napoli. Scored a brilliant individual goal in the 1958 World Cup in Sweden against West Germany in the

Famous names in the game

semi-final. Sweden lost 5-2 to Brazil in the final. Honours include a European Cup medal with AC Milan in 1969, a Cup Winners Cup medal for the same club in 1968 and one with Fiorentina in the same competition in 1961.

Herberger, Sepp

West Germany
Successful coach of the West German national side from 1936 to 1964 – for a total of 172 internationals. Previously played for Waldhof Mannheim and VFR Mannheim and won 3 caps. Highlight of his career was leading West Germany to their first World Cup victory in Switzerland in 1954, when they beat Hungary 3-2.

Herrera, Helenio

France
One of the most famous and best-paid coaches during the 1960s. He was at various times in charge of the French, Spanish and Italian national sides and took Inter Milan to victory in the European Cup in 1964 and 1965 – and the World Club championship in 1964. The South American was nicknamed 'slave driver'.

Keegan, Kevin

England
Transferred from Scunthorpe to Liverpool in 1971, Keegan's career blossomed as a striker. Voted English Footballer of the Year in 1976, he won league championship (1973, 1976 and 1977), European Cup (1977), UEFA Cup (1973 and 1976) and FA Cup (1974) awards with Liverpool. In 1977 he went to SV Hamburg, who won the German league title in 1979. He was voted European Footballer of the Year in 1978 and 1979 and returned to England in 1980 – to Southampton. He is currently captain of the England side.

Maier, Sepp

West Germany
In 1959, at the age of 15, Maier first played in goal for Bayern. Since 1966 he has won every award at world level and has played nearly 100 times for West Germany. In February 1978 he celebrated a West German League record of 400 consecutive appearances for his club. In 1978 in Argentina, Maier was West Germany's regular keeper for the third time in the World Cup.

Famous names in the game

Matthews, Sir Stanley

England

On 28 April 1965, Matthews played his last game in a British representative side against a World XI. He was then over 50. For more than 33 years this outside right made fools of defenders the world over. The Matthews trick has been imitated by many wing forwards since, but none have mastered it as skilfully as he did.

He started playing as a professional at the age of 17 and at 19 won the first of his 73 caps for England. Even at the age of 48, he played an important part in getting Stoke City into the First Division. The dribble expert, who was badly fouled again and again, was an example of fairness and sportsmanship throughout his playing career.

Merkel, Max

Austria

Merkel was one of the most successful coaches in Europe. This controversial 'Prussian from Vienna' was a hard task-master and often upset his players, but he certainly knew how to rouse players and sharpen them up at just the right time. His successes include a league championship medal with Rapid Vienna in 1957 as a player. As a coach his achievements include West German League runners-up with Borussia Dortmund in 1961; cup winners with Munich 1860 in 1964, European Cup Winners Cup runners-up in 1965 and West German champions in 1966; West German champions with 1st Nurenburg in 1968; and Spanish champions and cup winners with Atletico Madrid in 1973.

Moore, Bobby

England

Captained England's World Cup winning side of 1966. Previously he had led West Ham to the FA Cup in 1964 and the Cup Winners Cup in 1965. Voted English Footballer of the Year in 1964, he was the World Cup player of the tournament in 1966. He played in the 1962 World Cup and led England again in the 1970 World Cup. A cultured, calm defender, he went to Fulham in 1974 and retired from English football in 1977 after his 1000th game in top-class football. He went to the United States and played for Portland Timbers.

Muller, Gerd

West Germany

In 1964 the 'small fat man', as he was somewhat derogatively called, was transferred from TSV

Famous names in the game

Nordlingen to Bayern. Through his coach Tschik Cajkovsky, he established himself as one of the game's most prolific scorers. European Footballer of the Year in 1970, it was that year that he scored the most goals – 10 – in the World Cup. With Bayern he enjoyed league, cup and European Cup Winners Cup successes after 1966 and a European Cup medal in 1974. He gave up international soccer, then won two more European Cup medals before moving to the United States to play.

Pele
(Edson Arantes do Nascimento)

Brazil

The legendary Pele was probably the best player of all time. He was playing for the Brazilian club Santos at the age of 15 – and won his first cap for Brazil. He established himself as a world class player in the 1958 World Cup in Sweden, when only 18. From 1956 to 1968 he scored no fewer than 1200 goals for Santos and the Brazilian national team. Pele took part in four World Cups for Brazil, who won three of them (1958, 1962 and 1970).

He retired in 1974 but was persuaded to make a come-back for New York Cosmos the following year. He helped them to the league title and more than anyone prompted the soccer boom in the United States. He eventually retired in 1977.

Puskas, Ferenc

Hungary and Spain

Already a national player at the age of 17, he was capped for Hungary 82 times and was the star of the side that won 40 out of 47 internationals between 1951 and 1955, losing just one game – against West Germany in the 1954 World Cup Final in Berne.

He exiled himself from Hungary when touring with Honved in 1956 and joined Real Madrid two years later, forming an unforgettable partnership with Alfredo di Stefano. The 'Galloping Major' then played four times for Spain, including the 1962 World Cup. While with Real, he scored four goals against Eintracht Frankfurt in the 1960 European Cup Final.

In 1971 Puskas, then a manager, took the Greek club Panathinaikos to a European Cup final, which they lost 2-0 to Ajaz Amsterdam.

Rahn, Helmut

West Germany

This right winger won 40 caps for West Germany from 1951 to 1960

Famous names in the game

and scored the winning goal in the 1954 World Cup final in Berne against Hungary.

Ramsey, Sir Alf

England
Former manager of the England side, steering them to World Cup victory in 1966 and defeat in Mexico in 1970. Earlier he had taken Ipswich to the First Division championship (1962) from the Third Division in five seasons. As a Tottenham Hotspur player he had won Second and First Division championship medals in consecutive seasons. He also played for Southampton. He was knighted in 1967.

Rivera, Gianni

Italy
Led AC Milan to European Cup and World Club championship success in 1969; the same year he was voted European Footballer of the Year. This skilful midfield schemer was first capped in 1962 at the age of 18 and made his fourth appearance in the World Cup in 1974.

Schon, Helmut

West Germany
Succeeded Sepp Herberger as coach to the West German team in 1964, taking the national team to the World Cup final in England in 1966, where they lost 4-2 to England. Eight years later they became world champions with a 2-1 win over Holland, having finished third in the Mexico World Cup in 1970. Under him West Germany won the European Nations Cup in 1972 and were runners-up in 1976.

During his playing career, he proved himself one of the best forwards in the country between 1937 and 1941. He won 16 caps and scored 17 goals for his country.

Seeler, Uwe

West Germany
Before Muller, he was West Germany's top forward. From 1954, when he made his international debut against France at the age of 18, to the 1970 World Cup, when he opened up many opportunities for Muller in front of goal, he won 72 caps. He scored 43 goals and became the idol of German fans. In 1968 he led SV Hamburg to the European Cup Winners Cup final.

di Stefano, Alfredo

Argentina and Spain
This South American centre forward, who transferred from

Famous names in the game

River Plate (1942-49) via Millonarios (1950-52) and Barcelona (1953) to Real Madrid (1954-64) and finally to Espanol (1964-66), played seven times for Argentina and then won 31 caps for Spain. From 1956 to 1960 he was in the Real Madrid side that won the European Cup five times – and scored in every final. With him, Real won the league championship eight times and the cup once.

At this time di Stefano was considered the best player in the world. He was a great leader, strategist and fighter at a time when such world class players as Didi, Kopa and Simonsson were forced on to Real's substitute bench. He scored more than 500 goals for Real and was voted European Footballer of the Year in 1957 and again in 1959. In 1970 he was Argentina's Manager of the Year when in charge of Boca Juniors and the next season took Valencia to the Spanish league title.

Stein, Jock

Scotland
Led Celtic to a league and cup double in 1954, three years after playing non-league soccer in Wales. But he really made his mark as a manager, saving Dunfermline from relegation in 1960 and leading them to a cup triumph the following year. After a brief period with Hibernian, he was back at Celtic and from then on the awards flowed – league, cup and league cup – climaxed by Celtic's European Cup victory in 1967. He took over as Scotland's manager in 1978.

Walter, Fritz

West Germany
Walter played 61 times for West Germany between 1940 and 1958 and captained the side in the 1954 World Cup. He scored 33 goals for his country, putting himself behind only Seeler and Muller. He was regarded as Sepp Herberger's spokesman on the field, changing round and varying his coach's ideas. And even at the age of 37, he proved his athletic qualities in his last World Cup in Sweden in 1958.

Weisweiler, Hennes

West Germany
One of the most successful German soccer teachers, who 'made' an impressive list of world class players, including Vogts, Bonhof, Wimmer, Netzer and Heynkes for Borussia Monchengladbach. As a player for that club, he was in the league championship winning sides of 1970, 1971 and 1975 and the cup-winning team of 1973. He also

Famous names in the game

won a UEFA Cup medal in 1975. Since 1976 he has been coaching 1st Cologne. In 1977 and 1978 they won the national cup and completed the double in 1978 by winning the league as well.

Wright, Billy

England

First player to win 100 caps for England when he led the team against Scotland in 1959; he retired later that year with 105, having led England since 1948. Played more than 500 games for Wolves, leading them to victory in the FA Cup (1949) and the league (1954, 1958 and 1959). He was English Footballer of the Year in 1952. After he gave up playing he managed Arsenal from 1962 to 1966.

Yaschin, Lev

USSR

Regarded by many experts as the greatest goalkeeper of all time. For 20 uninterrupted years he played in goal for Moscow Dynamo. In 1963 he let through only 6 goals in 27 matches. He was capped 78 times for the USSR, won a gold medal in the Melbourne Olympics in 1956 and a winners medal in the 1960 European Nations Cup. He played for the USSR in four World Cups – in 1958, 1962, 1966 and 1970. In May 1971 – at the age of 42 – he played his last game in front of 103,000 spectators. And, for the record, in his career he saved more than 150 penalties.

Famous players in the United States

Alberto, Carlos

A native of Brazil, Alberto began his career in Rio at the age of 19. He has played more soccer games than any active player in the world, including more games as a team-mate of the great Pele than any other player. Known for his calm, cool style, he is able to trouble-shoot the most dangerous attacking situations. Carlos joined the New York Cosmos in 1977 and was voted Top Defender and first team All-Star in the following three years.

Chinaglia, Giorgio

Signed with the New York Cosmos from Italy in 1976, Giorgio is one of the greatest goal scorers in the history of the sport. His 1978 achievement of 34 goals and 79 points was a record for the greatest scoring in a regular season in league history. Holding every possible league goal-scoring record – for a game, for a season and for a career – Chinaglia also won the North American Soccer League's Most Valuable Player Award in 1981.

Cubillas, Teofilo

Born in Lima, Peru, 'Nene' began his professional career with Alianza-Lima at the age of 17. Before being signed by the Fort Lauderdale Strikers in 1979, he had a brilliant career in South America and Europe. His international record includes playing for Peru in two World Cup tournaments, where he was the second leading scorer in both matches, making him the fifth highest scorer in World Cup history. In his first year with Fort Lauderdale, Nene was a first team all – NASL selection and is now the leading league scorer.

Granitza, Karl-Heinz

Since his arrival from West Germany in 1978, Granitza has led the Chicago Sting goal-scoring drive. Although he began his soccer career as a defender, his thunderous left-footed shots and his ability to control the ball led him to become in 1981 only the fifth player in NASL history to score 200 points.

Mausser, Arnold

A native of Brooklyn, New York, Arnie Mausser is one of the premier goalkeepers in the NASL. Named North American Player of the Year and a first-team All Star in 1976, Mausser has the second most playing time in minutes of any NASL active goalkeeper. A U.S. National team selection for six consecutive years, he has more international experience than any American goalkeeper. Arnie joined the Jacksonville Team in 1980.

WESTERN RESERVE HIGH SCHOOL
LIBRARY